Copyright © 2023 by Jardine Publishing Ltd.

Published and written by Graham Jardine

Instagram: grahamjardinegolf

ISBN: 9798393904555

Illustration by Freepik

Manufactured in the United Kingdom

First Edition: May 2023

This book is dedicated to my dad, Sam, who started me on this journey buying me my first set of clubs all those years ago, my wife Lauren, a very patient golf widow, and my son, Joseph, I look forward to welcoming you to the game.

Navigating this book

WHY DO I LOVE THIS GAME?

CHAPTER 1

Foreword

When not playing well, it would be easy to ask yourself "Why do I love this game so much?" but put simply golf is a sport unlike any other. It is not just a game, but an art form that requires precision, technique, and focus. The beauty of golf is in its simplicity - a small white ball, a set of clubs, and a vast expanse of greenery. The challenge is not in the equipment, but in the mental and physical fortitude required to succeed. The sound of a well-struck shot, the satisfying feeling of sinking a putt, and the camaraderie of playing with friends - all of these factors contribute to my love of golf.

For me, golf is an escape from the stresses of everyday life. When I step onto the course, I leave behind the pressures of work and the demands of family. The fresh air, the beautiful scenery, and the sense of freedom that comes with being outdoors all contribute to a sense of peace and relaxation. Even on a bad day, a round of golf can leave me feeling rejuvenated and refreshed.

Golf is a sport that demands excellence. It is a game of inches, where a slight misjudgement can be the difference between a birdie and a bogey. The challenge of the game is what keeps me coming back. It is a never-ending quest for improvement, a constant battle against yourself. The thrill of hitting a great shot or achieving a personal best.

Golf is a sport that brings people together. Whether playing with friends, family, or strangers, the game fosters a sense of camaraderie and friendship. There is a shared love of the sport that transcends age, gender, and background. The golf course is a place where people can come together to enjoy the game, share stories, and build relationships.

Some of my fondest memories are on the golf course. From the first time I picked up a club as a child in my front garden with my sister, winning tournaments as a teenager, going to the driving range with my dad, returning to the game after many years break, winning tournaments as an adult or going to the final day at the 150th Open at St Andrews.

The game has also allowed me to meet new people, visit new places, and experience new cultures. The memories that golf has given me are priceless. I am now obsessed with every detail, the equipment, the cause and effect of subtle changes and the pursuit of perfection. There is no thrill like playing competitively. I am by no means a professional golfer, although I have often thought about it, I am a scratch golfer and who plays competitively at a regional level, and I have been studying this game for almost 25 years.

Unlike most I am self-taught, I have never had a lesson, and although this is not something to brag about, I have managed to work my way down to become a scratch golfer (some report this means I am somewhere between the top 2-5% of players worldwide). The only way I have been able to make this happen – is through trial and error. Continually reviewing the cause and effect of certain changes and taking a comprehensive set of notes. I decided to share these notes in this book and hopefully they help you take your game to the next level. I made this book small enough to fit in your bag as a constant source of direction when you feel like your game is lost.

In conclusion, there are many reasons why I love golf. The beauty of the game, the escape from reality, the challenge, the community, and the memories are all factors that make golf so addictive. It is a sport that requires skill, determination, and patience, but the rewards are immeasurable. Golf has given me so much and I look forward to many more years of playing this wonderful game.

SO, YOU WANT TO BE A GOLFER

CHAPTER 2

Why golf?

Golf is a sport that has captured the hearts and minds of millions of people around the world. From its health benefits to its social aspects, there are many factors that contribute to its addictive nature.

One of the most obvious reasons that golf is so addictive is the challenge it presents. Unlike other sports that may be more physically demanding, golf requires a great deal of mental and strategic skill. Golfers must navigate a course filled with obstacles such as bunkers, water hazards, and trees, and carefully plan their shots to avoid these obstacles and reach the green. The satisfaction of hitting a great shot and overcoming these challenges can be incredibly rewarding and drives golfers to keep playing and improving their game.

Another factor that contributes to golf's addictive nature is the social aspect of the sport. Golf is often played in groups, and golfers can meet and socialize with other players on the course. The time spent walking between holes and waiting for other players also provides a great opportunity for conversation and connection. Many golfers form lifelong friendships through the sport, and the social aspect can keep them coming back to the course even when their game isn't at its best.

One of the unique aspects of golf is that it can be played for a lifetime, making it a lifelong passion for many players. Unlike other sports that may become too physically demanding as players age, golf can be enjoyed by people of all ages and skill levels. This means that golfers can continue to play and improve their game throughout their lives, providing a sense of ongoing challenge and achievement.

In addition, golf is a sport that allows for self-improvement and personal growth. Because golf requires such a high level of mental and strategic skill, players must constantly evaluate and adjust their game to improve. This self-reflection and focus on improvement can translate to other areas of life, leading to personal growth and development.

Overall, the combination of challenge, socialization, lifelong playability, and personal growth make golf an incredibly addictive sport. Whether you're a seasoned pro or just starting out, the satisfaction of hitting a great shot and continually improving your game can keep you coming back to the course for years to come.

Recent boom in popularity

Golf has been a popular sport for centuries, but recently it has become even more popular, especially among younger generations. This increase in popularity can be attributed to various factors, such as technological advancements, media coverage, accessibility, and marketing strategies.

Advancements in golf technology, including high-tech golf clubs and balls, have made the game more enjoyable and accessible to players of all levels. Furthermore, media coverage has allowed fans to follow their favourite golfers and tournaments from anywhere in the world, thus increasing exposure and growth. Moreover, golf has become more accessible due to the development of more public courses, growth in golf tourism, and offering more affordable rates and flexible playing options.

Marketing strategies have also played a significant role in attracting younger generations to golf. The sport has become more inclusive and welcoming with campaigns focused on diversity and community building, and events and programs aimed at engaging and inspiring young people to start the game.

Social media has played a huge role in the recent popularity of golf. Platforms like Instagram and YouTube have given golfers the ability to share their swings, highlight reels, and trick shots with millions of people around the world. This exposure has brought new fans to the sport, as well as reignited the passion of existing golfers.

On the other hand, the recent surge in golf's popularity can also be attributed to the success of young players such as Tiger Woods and Rory McIlroy, and the growing interest in wellness and fitness. The success of these players has inspired a new generation of golfers to take up the game, while golf's physical and mental demands make it an attractive sport for people of all ages and backgrounds.

Another factor contributing to the popularity of golf is the growing interest in wellness and fitness. Golf is a sport that requires a high level of physical fitness and mental focus, making it a great way to stay healthy and reduce stress. This has made it an attractive sport for people of all ages and backgrounds, including those who may not have considered it before.

Finally, the accessibility of golf through technology and equipment has made it easier for people to get involved in the sport. Golf simulators and indoor driving ranges allow golfers to practice their swings and play rounds of golf from the comfort of their own homes.

In conclusion, golf's recent rise in popularity can be attributed to various factors, including technological advancements, media coverage, accessibility, marketing strategies, success of young players, and growing interest in wellness and fitness. As the sport continues to evolve and attract new fans, it is sure to remain a beloved pastime for years to come.

A brief history of golf

Golf is a sport that has a rich and fascinating history, originating in Scotland in the early 1400s. While its origins are somewhat uncertain, it is believed that the game evolved from a variety of ball-and-stick games that were played throughout Europe during the Middle Ages. Here are some important historical facts about golf:

1. The earliest recorded reference to golf dates back to 1457, when King James II of Scotland banned the game because he believed it was distracting his soldiers from practicing archery.

2. The first written rules of golf were established in 1744 by the Company of Gentlemen Golfers, which later became known as the Honourable Company of Edinburgh Golfers.

3. The first recorded golf tournament was held in 1766 at the Honourable Company of Edinburgh Golfers' course in Leith.

4. The first golf club in the United States was established in Charleston, South Carolina in 1786.

5. The modern game of golf as we know it today originated in Scotland in the mid-19th century, with the formation of the first golf clubs and the standardization of the rules.

6. The first Open Championship, now known as The Open, was held in 1860 at Prestwick Golf Club in Scotland and was won by Willie Park Sr.

7. The Masters Tournament, one of the four major championships in professional golf, was first played in 1934 at Augusta National Golf Club in Georgia.

8. The Ryder Cup, a biennial team competition between Europe and the United States, was first played in 1927 at Worcester Country Club in Massachusetts.

9. The Solheim Cup, a biennial team competition between women golfers from Europe and the United States, was first played in 1990.

10. Golf became an Olympic sport in 1900 but was later removed from the program after the 1904 Games. It was reintroduced in 2016, and Justin Rose of Great Britain won the gold medal in the men's individual event.

Over the centuries, golf has continued to adapt and evolve to changing times and cultures. Despite this, its core values of integrity, honesty, and sportsmanship have remained constant. Today, golf is enjoyed by millions of people around the world, ranging from amateur enthusiasts to professional players at the highest level of competition. Although the sport has undergone significant changes, it remains an essential part of our cultural heritage.

Since 1990, golf has experienced a number of significant moments and trends:

1. The Emergence of Tiger Woods: Tiger Woods' meteoric rise in the late 90s and early 2000s changed the game of golf, bringing it to a wider audience and inspiring a new generation of fans and players.

2. Technological Advances: Over the past few decades, golf equipment has evolved significantly, with new materials and designs resulting in longer distances and greater accuracy for players. The introduction of metal woods and high-tech golf balls has been particularly impactful.

3. Expansion of the Golf Industry: Golf has become a multi-billion-dollar industry, with a vast array of products and services catering to players and enthusiasts alike. The globalization of the sport has opened up new markets and opportunities for growth.

4. Inclusion and Diversity: Golf has traditionally been dominated by white male players, but recent years have seen efforts to promote diversity and inclusion in the sport. Initiatives such as promoting women's and junior golf and making golf more accessible to people from different backgrounds and abilities, have been key in this regard.

5. Changes in Rules and Formats: Golf's governing bodies have made several changes to the rules and formats of the game, with the aim of speeding up play and reducing the use of technology. New formats such as the Ryder Cup and the WGC-Dell Technologies Match Play have also been introduced.

6. Challenges and Opportunities: Golf has faced challenges in recent years, including declining participation rates and the impact of the COVID-19 pandemic. However, the use of new technologies and the potential inclusion of golf in the Olympics present exciting opportunities for the sport's future. Overall, golf continues to evolve and adapt to changing times and cultures, while its core principles of integrity, honesty, and sportsmanship remain constant. Despite the challenges it has faced, the sport remains beloved by millions of people around the world.

The game of golf has seen significant changes and developments since 2020, with notable events and trends that have shaped the sport. These include:

1. Impact of COVID-19: The COVID-19 pandemic has had a major impact on golf, causing the cancellation or postponement of many events and leading to new safety protocols and guidelines for players, caddies, and staff.

2. Bryson DeChambeau's Dominance: American golfer Bryson DeChambeau emerged as a dominant player on the PGA Tour, thanks to his unique approach that combines bulk, power, and scientific methods to optimize his swing and ball flight.

3. Increased Focus on Diversity and Inclusion: In response to social justice movements, the golf industry has emphasized diversity and inclusion, with initiatives and organizations established to promote golf among underrepresented groups.

4. Innovation in Equipment and Technology: The golf industry continues to innovate, with smart golf clubs and environmentally sustainable courses among the latest developments.

5. Rise of Women's Golf: Women's golf has seen significant growth and development, with the LPGA Tour expanding globally and the introduction of the Augusta National Women's Amateur.

6. Golf's Return to the Olympics: Golf's return to the Olympics in 2016 and continued inclusion in the Games is hoped to grow the game and inspire a new generation of golfers worldwide.

How is this changing the culture of golf?

The culture of golf has undergone significant changes in recent years, as the sport has worked to modernize and appeal to a broader audience. Some of the key changes in the culture of golf include:

Increased diversity

Golf has historically been seen as a sport for wealthy, white men, but efforts to increase diversity and inclusion in the game are starting to pay off. Women, people of colour, and players from different socioeconomic backgrounds are all becoming more involved in golf, both as players and fans.

Emphasis on fitness

Golf is no longer seen as a leisurely pastime for retirees, but rather as a sport that requires physical fitness and athleticism. Many golfers now incorporate strength and conditioning training into their routines, and courses are being designed with more challenging terrain and longer distances to reflect this shift.

Use of technology

Technology is increasingly being used in golf to improve performance and make the game more accessible. GPS tracking systems, swing analysers, and other digital tools are all being used to help golfers improve their game and get more out of their time on the course.

Sustainability and conservation

Golf courses have traditionally been criticized for their environmental impact, but many courses are now adopting more sustainable practices to reduce their footprint. This includes using organic fertilizers, conserving water, and planting native vegetation to support local ecosystems.

Casualization of attire

Golf has historically been a sport with strict dress codes, but many courses are now relaxing their rules to allow for more casual and comfortable attire. This reflects a broader shift in culture towards a more relaxed and inclusive approach to dress.

All of these changes are helping to make golf a more dynamic and accessible sport, with a culture that is more welcoming to a diverse range of players and fans. As golf continues to evolve, it will be interesting to see how these trends continue to shape the game and its culture. Additionally, the pandemic has accelerated some of these changes, as golfers have had to adapt to new protocols and ways of playing the game. The pandemic has also highlighted the importance of outdoor activities and provided an opportunity for golf to attract new players who are looking for a safe and socially distant form of recreation. As such, the culture of golf is likely to continue evolving in exciting ways in the years to come.

The constant pursuit of perfection

Golf has a rich history that spans centuries, and its addictive nature has been documented throughout the ages. In fact, Scottish Kings were so concerned about their subjects spending too much time playing golf that they banned the sport by royal decree in the 15th century. Despite this early attempt at regulation, the allure of golf has only grown stronger over time, as players around the world continue to be drawn to the sport's unique combination of skill, precision, and finesse.

Golf is a game of skill, precision, and finesse. It is a game that requires a great deal of practice, patience, and persistence. Golfers who have reached the pinnacle of the sport have done so through years of dedication, hard work, and a relentless pursuit of perfection.

Perfection in golf is not an attainable goal, but rather a pursuit. It is the constant striving to improve one's skills and technique, to play to the best of one's ability, and to minimize errors and mistakes. The pursuit of perfection in golf is a journey that never truly ends, and even the best golfers in the world continue to work on their games to stay at the top of their sport.

While the idea of achieving perfection in golf may seem unattainable, it is the relentless pursuit of excellence that has driven some of the greatest players in history to achieve extraordinary feats on the course. From Tiger Woods to Jack Nicklaus, the world's top golfers have dedicated countless hours to perfecting their swings, developing mental toughness, and seeking out feedback from coaches and peers.

One of the key elements of the pursuit of perfection in golf is practice. Golfers must practice their swings, short game, and putting to develop the skills and technique necessary to compete at the highest level. Practice is not only about repetition but also about quality, focusing on the small details, and addressing weaknesses in one's game.

Another important element in the pursuit of perfection is mental toughness. Golf is a mentally demanding sport, and the ability to stay focused, remain calm under pressure, and stay committed to the task at hand is essential. Golfers must develop a positive mindset, visualize success, and stay present in the moment to perform their best.

It is also important for golfers to seek out feedback and guidance from experienced coaches, mentors, or other golfers. Learning from others can help golfers identify areas for improvement and refine their technique. Feedback can also help golfers stay motivated and accountable in their pursuit of perfection.

But the pursuit of perfection can also be a double-edged sword. While it can motivate golfers to push themselves to new heights, it can also create immense pressure and lead to frustration and disappointment when mistakes inevitably happen. That's why it's important for golfers to balance their drive for perfection with self-compassion, resilience, and a willingness to accept their imperfections.

Ultimately, the pursuit of perfection in golf is a never-ending journey that requires dedication, hard work, mental toughness, and a willingness to seek feedback and guidance. It is the pursuit of excellence that drives golfers to continue striving to be their best on the course, no matter the obstacles they face along the way.

HOW DO I GET INTO GOLF?

CHAPTER 3

Entry Points

Golf is a unique sport that can be played by people of all ages and abilities. It is a game that requires skill, patience, and practice to excel. Golf is played on a course with 18 holes, each hole being a different challenge for the player.

Learning to play golf at a young age can have many benefits. First and foremost, it provides an opportunity to develop fundamental skills and techniques early on, which can be beneficial for long-term growth and success in the sport. Additionally, starting young can help instil a love and appreciation for the game, which can lead to a lifelong passion for golf. It can also provide a unique and enjoyable way to spend time outdoors and get exercise, promoting physical activity and healthy habits. Finally, learning golf at a young age can help develop important life skills such as discipline, patience, and perseverance, which can be applied in all areas of life.

The flip side is that many people start playing golf as adults, often after being introduced to the sport by a friend or family member. Others may become interested in golf after attending a corporate outing or charity event. To start playing golf as an adult, one typically needs to join a club or find a public course where they can take lessons or practice on their own. Some beginners may feel intimidated or self-conscious when they first start playing, but with patience, persistence, and guidance from experienced golfers or instructors, they can develop the skills and confidence necessary to enjoy the sport. Adult beginners may also benefit from using beginner-friendly equipment, such as clubs with larger clubheads or softer golf balls, to help them get the ball in the air and make solid contact. Ultimately, the key to starting golf as an adult is to have a willingness to learn, a positive attitude, and a desire to have fun on the course.

In recent years, the popularity of golf has been on the rise, and people are entering the sport in various ways.

Junior Golf

Junior golf programs are becoming more popular, and more and more children are getting involved in the sport. Junior golf programs provide an excellent opportunity for children to learn the game, develop their skills, and make new friends. These programs are typically run by golf clubs or local golf associations and provide an environment where children can learn in a safe and fun setting. It provides a skill for life and often junior golfers return to the sport in later life, retaining a lot of the skills they developed.

College Golf

College golf is another entry point for many golfers. College golf teams provide an opportunity for players to compete at a higher level while obtaining an education. College golfers also have the opportunity to receive scholarships, which can help pay for their education.

Corporate Golf

Corporate golf is becoming more popular as companies use golf as a way to build relationships with clients and employees. Many companies now host golf tournaments, where employees can compete against each other or play with clients.

Corporate golf events provide an excellent opportunity for people to network and build relationships in a relaxed and enjoyable setting.

Retirement Golf

Many people start golf in retirement as a way to stay active and socialize with others. Golf provides an opportunity to spend time outdoors, enjoy the scenery, and get some exercise. Retirement golf is also a great way to meet new people and make new friends.

Recreational Golf

Recreational golf is the most popular entry point for most golfers. It involves playing golf for fun and enjoyment with friends and family. Recreational golfers play on public courses, which are accessible to everyone, and can be played at any time.

Golf is a sport that can be played at any age and ability level, and there are many entry points to the game. Junior golf programs, college golf, corporate golf, retirement golf, and recreational golf are all ways to get involved in the sport. Whether you are looking to compete at a high level or just play for fun, golf provides an opportunity to enjoy the outdoors, get some exercise, and make new friends.

The great equaliser: Understanding the Handicap System in Golf

Golf is a unique sport in that players of different skill levels can compete against each other on an equal footing, thanks to the handicap system. The handicap system is a way to level the playing field by giving weaker players a stroke advantage based on their skill level. In this chapter, we will explore the basics of the handicap system and how it works.

What is a handicap?

A golf handicap is a numerical measure of a golfer's playing ability. The higher the handicap, the less skilled the player is considered to be. A handicap is calculated based on a golfer's past scores and the difficulty of the course they are playing.

How is a handicap calculated?

To calculate a golfer's handicap, their scores from recent rounds of golf are used. The formula considers the golfer's best scores, while also factoring in the difficulty of the course they played on. The result is a number that represents the golfer's playing ability.

How does the handicap system work?

The handicap system is designed to allow golfers of different skill levels to compete against each other. The system works by giving weaker players a stroke advantage based on their handicap. For example, if a golfer with a handicap of 18 is playing against a golfer with a handicap of 8, the weaker player would receive 10 strokes to level the playing field.

The handicap system is also used to determine the number of strokes a player should receive on each hole. This is based on the difficulty of the hole, with more difficult holes giving weaker players more strokes.

Why is the handicap system important?

The handicap system is important because it allows golfers of different skill levels to compete against each other. Without a handicap system, weaker players would have little chance of winning against stronger players. Additionally, the handicap system allows players to track their progress and improvement over time, providing motivation to continue practicing and improving their game.

In conclusion, the handicap system is an essential part of golf that allows players of different skill levels to compete against each other. Understanding how the handicap system works is important for anyone who wants to play golf competitively or simply wants to track their own progress over time.

Exploring the Different Formats of Golf

Golf is a sport that can be played in many different ways, from individual stroke play to team events. In this chapter, we will explore the different formats of golf and their unique characteristics.

Stroke Play

Stroke play is the most common format of golf. In this format, each player plays their own ball and the player with the lowest total score at the end of the round is the winner. Stroke play is used in most professional golf tournaments and many amateur events.

Match Play

Match play is a format where players compete against each other, rather than against the entire field. In match play, each hole is a separate competition, and the player with the lowest score on each hole wins that hole. The player who wins the most holes is the winner of the match. Match play is often used in team events, such as the Ryder Cup.

Stableford

The Stableford format is a points-based system that rewards players for good scores on each hole. Players are awarded points based on their net score on each hole, with higher points for lower scores. The player with the most points at the end of the round is the winner.

Skins

Skins is a format where each hole is a separate competition, and the player with the lowest score on each hole wins a "skin." The value of each skin is determined by the players before the round. The player with the most skins at the end of the round is the winner.

Scramble

A scramble is a team event where each player hits a tee shot, and the team chooses the best shot. All players then hit their second shot from the spot of the chosen shot, and the process is repeated until the ball is holed. Scrambles are often used in charity events and corporate outings.

Best Ball

Best ball is a team event where each player plays their own ball, and the lowest score on each hole is counted as the team score. This format is often used in team events and is popular among golfers of all skill levels.

Four-Ball

Four-ball is a team event where each player plays their own ball, and the lowest score on each hole is counted as the team score. However, in four-ball, each player is paired with a partner, and the team with the lowest combined score is the winner.

In conclusion, golf is a versatile sport that can be played in many different formats. Each format has its own unique characteristics and is suited to different types of players and events. Understanding the different formats of golf is important for anyone who wants to play competitively or simply wants to try new ways of playing the game.

The Role of a Professional Coach

A golf instructor plays an important role in helping golfers improves their game. A good instructor should have a deep understanding of the fundamentals of the game, as well as experience working with golfers of all levels. They should be able to provide clear, concise feedback on technique and offer personalized instruction to meet the unique needs of each golfer.

In addition to teaching technique, a good golf instructor should also be able to provide guidance on course management, mental preparation, and other aspects of the game. They should be able to help golfers set goals, track progress, and develop a plan for long-term improvement.

The Importance of Proper Technique Proper technique is essential to success in golf. Without proper technique, golfers may struggle with accuracy, distance, and consistency. Even experienced golfers can benefit from a refresher on the basics of proper technique.

Some of the key aspects of proper technique include a strong grip, correct stance and posture, proper alignment, and a smooth, fluid swing. It is important for golfers to work with an instructor to ensure they are using proper technique and to make adjustments as needed.

Golf instruction is an essential component of improving your skills on the course. In this chapter, we covered the benefits of golf instruction, the role of a golf instructor, and the importance of proper technique. By developing a strong foundation in the fundamentals of the game, you can improve your performance, prevent injury, and enjoy the game of golf to the fullest.

In addition to improving your physical skills, golf instruction can also help you develop mental skills that are essential to success on the course. This includes things like focus, patience, and a positive attitude. By working with an experienced instructor, you can learn strategies for staying calm and focused under pressure, managing your emotions on the course, and maintaining a positive outlook, even in the face of adversity.

It is important to note that while golf instruction can be incredibly helpful, it is not a substitute for practice and dedication. The best golfers are those who put in the time and effort to refine their skills and develop a deep understanding of the game.

Finally, it is important to remember that golf is a game, and it should be enjoyed as such. While the pursuit of improvement and success is important, it is also important to have fun and enjoy the process. By approaching the game with a sense of joy and enthusiasm, you can cultivate a love for golf that will last a lifetime.

Taking the hard path... Teaching Yourself

Golf is a sport that can be played and enjoyed by people of all ages and skill levels. However, many beginners may find it daunting to start the game, as it requires patience, practice, and precision. While it is recommended to take lessons from a professional golf coach, it is also possible to teach yourself golf and learn at your own pace. Here are some tips on teaching yourself golf:

1. Start with the basics: Before hitting the golf course, it is important to learn the fundamentals of the game. This includes understanding the equipment, such as the clubs and the ball, as well as the rules and etiquette of the game. You can find instructional videos and articles online or check out books from the library.

2. Practice, practice, practice: Golf is a game that requires repetition and consistency. To improve your skills, you need to practice regularly. Find a driving range or practice facility where you can hit balls and work on your swing. You can also practice putting at home with a putting mat or in your backyard.

3. Play with others: While practicing alone is important, playing with others is also essential for improving your game. Join a golf league or find a group of friends to play with. You can also play in a casual setting, such as a mini-golf course, to get more comfortable with the game.

4. Focus on one aspect at a time: Golf is a complex game that involves multiple skills, such as driving, chipping, and putting. It can be overwhelming to try to improve all of these skills at once. Instead, focus on one aspect at a time and work on improving it before moving on to the next.

5. Embrace the learning process: Golf is a challenging sport, and it takes time to improve. Embrace the learning process and enjoy the journey. Don't get discouraged if you hit a bad shot or have a bad round. Keep practicing and have fun.

In my experience teaching yourself golf can be a rewarding experience. By following these tips, you can learn at your own pace and enjoy the game of golf for years to come. This will take a long time and can often results in bad habits.

Whichever method you choose, it is important to remember that golf is a game, and it should be enjoyed as such. While the pursuit of improvement and success is important, it is also important to have fun and enjoy the process. By approaching the game with a sense of joy and enthusiasm, you can cultivate a love for golf that will last a lifetime.

In the following chapters, we will cover everything from the basics of golf technique to advanced strategies for course management and mental preparation. Whether you're a beginner or an experienced golfer, there is something in this book for you. So, grab your clubs and let's get started on the path to improving your game!

UNDERSTANDING GOLF EQUIPMENT

CHAPTER 4

Equipment, Equipment, Equipment

Having the right golf equipment is crucial for playing your best game. In this chapter, we will explore the different types of golf equipment and how to choose the right equipment for your game.

Golf clubs are the most important piece of equipment for golfers. There are several types of clubs, including drivers, irons, wedges, and putters. Each type of club has a specific purpose, and choosing the right club for each shot is essential for improving your game. It is important to have a set of clubs that fit your swing and your physical characteristics, such as your height and arm length.

Golf balls come in a variety of types and styles, and choosing the right ball for your game can make a significant difference in your performance. There are different types of golf balls for different types of swings, such as low spin, high spin, and distance balls. It is important to choose a ball that fits your swing and your playing style.

Golf shoes are designed to provide traction and stability on the course. They come in several styles, including spiked and spikeless shoes. It is important to choose a comfortable and supportive shoe that fits well and provides the necessary traction for your swing.

There are several other golf accessories that can improve your game, such as gloves, hats, rangefinders, and golf GPS devices. These accessories can help you stay comfortable and focused on the course and improve your accuracy and distance.

Having the right golf equipment is essential for playing your best game. In this chapter, we explored the different types of golf equipment, including golf clubs, golf balls, and other golf accessories. By choosing equipment that fits your swing and your playing style, you can improve your performance and enjoy the game more fully.

Custom fitting vs off the shelf

When it comes to buying golf clubs, there are two main options: buying off the shelf or going through the custom fitting process. While there are pros and cons to each approach, the case for custom fitting is strong.

Firstly, custom fitting allows for a more personalized experience. A qualified club fitter can consider a golfer's individual swing characteristics, physical attributes, and preferences to create a set of clubs that are tailored to their needs. This level of personalization simply isn't possible with off-the-shelf clubs.

Secondly, custom fitting can help golfers achieve greater performance on the course. When a club is customized to a golfer's individual needs, they may see improvements in accuracy, distance, and consistency. This is because the club will be optimized to their individual swing, resulting in better ball flight and greater control.

Thirdly, custom fitting can actually save money in the long run. While custom clubs may be more expensive upfront, the improved performance they provide can actually help golfers avoid having to purchase new clubs as frequently. Additionally, custom fitting can help golfers avoid costly mistakes, such as purchasing clubs that aren't suited to their swing or physical attributes.

On the other hand, buying off the shelf does offer some benefits. It can be less expensive than custom fitting, and it allows golfers to purchase clubs immediately rather than having to wait for a fitting appointment. Additionally, off-the-shelf clubs may work well for golfers with relatively average swing characteristics and physical attributes.

However, the advantages of custom fitting typically outweigh the advantages of buying off the shelf. Custom fitting allows for a more personalized experience, better performance on the course, and can actually save golfers money in the long run.

In summary, while there are pros and cons to both approaches, the case for custom fitting is strong. Custom fitting allows for a more personalized experience, better performance on the course, and can even save golfers money in the long run. While buying off the shelf may be less expensive and more convenient, it simply doesn't offer the same level of personalization and performance optimization that custom fitting does. It is recommended that you do multiple fittings to ensure you don't 'bring a bad swing' into your new clubs.

Selecting you putter

Choosing the right putter is critical to your success on the greens. With so many different putters on the market, it can be difficult to determine which one is best suited for your game. Here are some factors to consider when selecting the right putter for you:

1. Length: The length of the putter is one of the most important factors to consider. The length of the putter should be comfortable and promote a consistent, repeatable stroke. Putter lengths typically range from 32 to 36 inches, with longer putters being better suited for golfers with taller stances.

2. Head design: The shape of the putter head can also have a significant impact on your putting stroke. Mallet putters tend to be more forgiving and offer better alignment aids, while blade putters offer a more traditional look and feel. Golfers with an arced putting stroke may prefer blade putters, while those with a straight back-and-forth motion may prefer mallet putters.

3. Weight: The weight of the putter is another important consideration. A heavier putter can help promote a smoother stroke and reduce the effects of hand and wrist movement. However, a lighter putter may be better for golfers with slower swing speeds or those who struggle with distance control.

4. Grip: The grip of the putter can also have a significant impact on your putting stroke. A thicker grip can help reduce wrist action and promote a more stable stroke, while a thinner grip may be better for golfers who prefer a lighter feel.

5.   Custom fitting: Working with a qualified club fitter can help you determine the ideal putter for your game. A fitter can assess your putting stroke and recommend putters with the right length, weight, and head design to maximize your performance on the greens.

Ultimately, the right putter is the one that feels comfortable and allows you to make a consistent, repeatable stroke. Experimenting with different putters and working with a qualified instructor or club fitter can help you find the putter that works best for your game. Remember, putting is all about confidence and trust, so choose a putter that inspires confidence and feels great in your hands.

Selecting your wedges

Wedges are one of the most important clubs in a golfer's bag, and choosing the right loft and bounce can have a significant impact on your ability to hit a variety of shots around the green. The loft and bounce of a wedge are closely related, and understanding how they work together can help you choose the right wedge for your game.

Loft refers to the angle of the clubface, with higher lofted wedges having a steeper angle than lower lofted clubs. Typically, wedges come in a variety of lofts, ranging from 46 degrees to 64 degrees or higher. Choosing the right loft for your wedges depends on a number of factors, including your swing speed, course conditions, and the types of shots you prefer to play.

In general, the higher the loft of the wedge, the more spin and height you can generate on your shots, making them ideal for short, high shots around the green. Lower lofted wedges, on the other hand, are better suited for full shots and longer distances.

Bounce refers to the angle between the leading edge of the clubface and the sole of the club. Bounce is important because it helps prevent the club from digging too deeply into the turf, which can cause fat or thin shots. Wedges typically come in a variety of bounce angles, ranging from low bounce (4-6 degrees) to high bounce (12-14 degrees or more).

The amount of bounce you need depends on the course conditions you typically play on and your own swing characteristics. Golfers who play on firm, fast courses typically benefit from wedges with lower bounce, as they allow for more versatility and better control on tight lies. Golfers who play on softer courses or have a steeper angle of attack on their shots may benefit from wedges with higher bounce, as they help prevent the club from digging too deeply into the turf.

Ultimately, the best way to select the right wedge loft and bounce is to experiment with different options on the course or at the range. Pay attention to the types of shots you typically play and the conditions you play in and choose wedges that allow you to hit a variety of shots with confidence and consistency. Additionally, working with a qualified instructor or club fitter can help you make more informed decisions about the wedges that will work best for your game.

Selecting the right irons

When it comes to selecting the right irons for your game, there are two main categories to consider: blades and cavity-backs.

Blades, also known as muscle-backs, are traditional-style irons that have a small clubhead with a thin top line and minimal offset. These irons are typically designed for advanced golfers with a consistent, repeatable swing. Blades offer greater shot-making ability and precision but require a higher level of skill to hit consistently.

Cavity-back irons, on the other hand, have a larger clubhead with a hollowed-out cavity behind the clubface. This design allows for more forgiveness on off-centre hits and a lower centre of gravity, which can help golfers get the ball airborne more easily. Cavity-back irons are generally more forgiving and easier to hit than blades, making them a good choice for intermediate and beginner golfers.

When selecting the right irons for your game, there are several factors to consider:

1. Skill level: As mentioned, blades are designed for advanced golfers who have a consistent, repeatable swing. If you're a beginner or intermediate player, you may find cavity-back irons to be more forgiving and easier to hit.

2. Ball flight: Blades are typically designed to produce a lower ball flight, which can be advantageous in windy conditions. Cavity-back irons, on the other hand, tend to launch the ball higher, which can help golfers hit longer shots and hold greens more easily.

3. Shot-making ability: If you're a golfer who likes to shape shots and hit precise distances, blades may be a better choice for you. Cavity-back irons are designed for straighter, more forgiving shots.

4. Feel: Blades offer a softer, more muted feel at impact, which can be appealing to some golfers. Cavity-back irons tend to offer a more solid, responsive feel.

5. Custom fitting: Working with a qualified club fitter can help you determine the ideal irons for your game. A fitter can assess your swing and recommend irons with the right shaft, length, and head design to maximize your performance on the course.

Ultimately, the right irons for your game will depend on your individual needs and preferences. If you're an advanced golfer with a consistent swing, you may find that blades offer greater shot-making ability and precision. If you're a beginner or intermediate player looking for more forgiveness and ease of use, cavity-back irons may be a better choice. Working with a qualified club fitter can help ensure that you find the irons that work best for your game.

Selecting your driver

The driver is often considered the most important club in a golfer's bag, as it sets the tone for the entire round. Selecting the right driver can be a daunting task, as there are many factors to consider, including distance and forgiveness.

When it comes to distance, golfers often look for a driver that can maximize their yardage off the tee. This usually involves selecting a driver with a larger clubhead, a longer shaft, and a lower loft angle. However, it's important to note that maximizing distance may come at the cost of forgiveness.

Forgiveness, on the other hand, refers to a driver's ability to minimize the negative effects of off-centre hits. This is typically achieved through a driver with a larger clubhead, a higher moment of inertia (MOI), and a greater amount of perimeter weighting. A more forgiving driver can help golfers hit straighter shots, even when they miss the centre of the clubface.

So, how do you strike a balance between distance and forgiveness when selecting a driver?

First, consider your own swing. If you have a consistent, repeatable swing and can consistently find the centre of the clubface, a driver with a smaller clubhead and lower loft angle may help you achieve greater distance. However, if you struggle with consistency and tend to miss the centre of the clubface, a driver with a larger clubhead and higher MOI may be a better choice for you.

Second, consider the course conditions you typically play in. If you frequently play on courses with narrow fairways and hazards, forgiveness may be a higher priority for you. If you play on courses with more open fairways and opportunities for long drives, distance may be a greater consideration.

Finally, take advantage of custom fitting. Working with a qualified club fitter can help you find a driver with the right shaft, loft angle, and head design to optimize your performance on the course. A fitter can also help you strike the right balance between distance and forgiveness, ensuring that you find a driver that fits your individual needs and preferences.

In summary, selecting the right driver involves striking a balance between distance and forgiveness. Consider your swing, the course conditions you typically play in, and take advantage of custom fitting to find a driver that works best for your game.

Critical Step - Shaft Flex

The shaft choice is arguably the most critical component of a golf club that can significantly impact a golfer's swing and ball flight. The flex of a golf club refers to its ability to bend when a golfer swings it, and is typically classified as extra stiff, stiff, regular, or senior, with variations in between. Each flex has its own characteristics and can impact a golfer's game in different ways.

The shaft of a golf club plays a critical role in determining the accuracy, distance, and overall performance of a golfer's swing. If a golfer's shaft is too stiff, it can result in a lack of distance, as the clubhead fails to transfer energy effectively to the ball. Additionally, a stiff shaft can make it difficult to achieve the proper launch angle and spin rate, leading to inconsistent ball flight and accuracy. On the other hand, a shaft that is too flexible can cause the clubhead to close too quickly at impact, resulting in a hook or a slice. This can lead to a loss of distance and accuracy, as well as increased frustration for the golfer. Ultimately, finding the right shaft stiffness is crucial to maximizing a golfer's potential and achieving consistent, high-quality shots on the course.

Extra stiff shafts are the least flexible and are typically used by golfers with the highest swing speeds. These shafts require a lot of power to bend, and as a result, they tend to provide less spin and a lower trajectory. Extra stiff shafts are ideal for golfers who are looking for maximum distance and control, but they can be challenging to use for those who don't generate enough swing speed to activate the flex.

Stiff shafts are slightly more flexible than extra stiff shafts and are often used by golfers with moderate to high swing speeds. These shafts offer a balance of control and distance, providing enough flex to generate spin and launch the ball higher while still maintaining accuracy. Stiff shafts are a popular choice for many golfers, as they provide a good compromise between power and precision.

Regular shafts are the most common flex and are suitable for golfers with moderate swing speeds. These shafts are flexible enough to provide good spin and launch, but not so flexible that they sacrifice control or accuracy. Regular shafts are a versatile option that can work well for many golfers, but they may not be suitable for those with very fast or slow swing speeds.

Senior shafts are the most flexible option and are typically used by golfers with slower swing speeds. These shafts are designed to bend easily and generate maximum spin and height, but they may sacrifice some distance and control in the process. Senior shafts are ideal for golfers who are looking to maximize their distance while still maintaining accuracy.

Overall, the choice of shaft flex can have a significant impact on a golfer's game, and it's important to choose a shaft that matches your swing speed and playing style. Consulting with a professional fitter or coach can help you determine which shaft flex is best for your game, and experimenting with different options can help you fine-tune your performance on the course.

Critical Step - Grip Sizes

The grip is the only point of contact between a golfer and the club, making it a crucial factor in determining how a player performs on the course. One of the key elements of a grip is its size, which can have a significant impact on a golfer's swing and ball flight and is often an afterthought even in professional fittings.

The size of a grip is determined by its diameter, with smaller diameters providing a tighter grip and larger diameters offering a looser grip. Grips are typically classified as standard, midsize, or oversized, with variations in between. Each grip size has its own characteristics and can affect a golfer's game in different ways.

Standard grips are the most common size and are suitable for most golfers. They provide a neutral feel and can work well for golfers with average-sized hands. Standard grips offer a balance of control and comfort and are typically used by golfers who prefer a traditional feel.

Midsize grips are slightly larger in diameter than standard grips and are ideal for golfers with larger hands. These grips provide a more relaxed and comfortable feel and can help golfers maintain a lighter grip pressure while still maintaining control. Midsize grips are also popular among golfers who suffer from arthritis or other hand injuries.

Oversized grips are the largest size and are suitable for golfers who struggle with hand fatigue or tend to grip the club too tightly. These grips offer maximum comfort and can help golfers reduce their grip pressure, resulting in a smoother and more consistent swing. Oversized grips can also help golfers who tend to slice the ball, as they promote a more neutral hand position at impact.

Choosing the right grip size is important for maximizing performance on the course. A grip that is too small can cause golfers to grip the club too tightly, resulting in a tense and erratic swing, while a grip that is too large can cause golfers to lose control and accuracy. Consultation with a professional fitter or coach can help golfers determine which grip size is best for their game and ensure that they are getting the most out of their clubs.

Critical Step - Don't forget your Golf ball!

The golf ball is a crucial piece of equipment for any golfer, and choosing the right ball can have a significant impact on a player's performance on the course. While golf balls may look similar on the surface, there are actually many different types of balls available, each with its own unique characteristics and performance benefits.

One of the most important factors to consider when choosing a golf ball is its compression. Compression refers to the density of the ball and is typically rated on a scale of 0-200. Lower compression balls are softer and more forgiving, making them ideal for golfers with slower swing speeds or those who struggle with accuracy. Higher compression balls are harder and offer more distance and control, making them better suited for golfers with faster swing speeds or those who need more accuracy.

Another important consideration is the ball's cover material. Most golf balls today feature either a urethane or surlyn cover. Urethane covers offer greater spin control and feel, making them a popular choice for better players. Surlyn covers, on the other hand, are more durable and provide greater distance and forgiveness, making them a good choice for beginners and high-handicap players.

Other factors to consider when choosing a golf ball include its dimple pattern, which can affect the ball's trajectory and spin, and its overall construction, which can impact its durability and feel.

Choosing the right golf ball is important for maximizing performance on the course. A ball that is too soft or hard for your swing speed can lead to inconsistent shots and reduced distance, while a ball with the wrong cover material can negatively impact spin and feel. Additionally, using the same type of ball consistently can help golfers develop a feel and consistency with their shots, which can lead to improved performance over time.

In conclusion, while it may be tempting to simply grab any golf ball off the shelf, taking the time to choose the right ball can have a significant impact on your performance on the course. Consider your individual needs and preferences, and experiment with different types of balls to find the one that works best for your game. With the right ball, you can improve your accuracy, distance, and overall enjoyment of the game.

Developing an intimate understanding of your clubs

Developing knowledge about golf clubs can greatly enhance a golfer's performance on the course. Knowing the different types of clubs, their functions, and how they are designed can help golfers make more informed decisions about which clubs to use in different situations.

There are several different types of golf clubs, each designed for a specific purpose. These include drivers, fairway woods, hybrids, irons, wedges, and putters. Drivers are designed for long shots off the tee, while fairway woods and hybrids are often used for long shots from the fairway or rough. Irons are used for a variety of different shots, including approach shots to the green, while wedges are designed for shots requiring a high degree of accuracy and control, such as bunker shots or chips around the green. Putters are used for shots on the green and are designed to roll the ball smoothly and accurately.

Golf clubs are also designed with different features, such as loft, shaft length, and clubhead design. Loft refers to the angle of the clubface, which affects the trajectory and distance of the ball. Shafts can vary in length, flex, and material, which can affect the speed and accuracy of the swing. Clubhead design can vary, with some clubs having a larger sweet spot for increased forgiveness, while others have a smaller sweet spot for increased control.

To develop knowledge about golf clubs, it's important to research and understand the different features and designs of each club. This can involve reading articles and reviews, consulting with a club fitter or golf professional, and experimenting with different clubs on the range or course. It's also important to consider individual preferences and playing style when selecting clubs, as what works for one golfer may not work for another.

Developing knowledge about golf clubs can help golfers make better decisions on the course, leading to improved performance and greater enjoyment of the game. By understanding the different types of clubs and their features, golfers can select the right club for each shot and feel confident in their ability to execute the shot.

Remember If it Ain't broke...

There is a common belief among many golfers that buying new and improved golf equipment will automatically lead to better performance on the course. However, the reality is that simply upgrading your equipment will not necessarily translate to lower scores or improved performance. In fact, the saying "if it isn't broke, don't fix it" applies to golf equipment as well.

While new equipment may offer certain technological advancements or improvements in design, the impact of these improvements on a golfer's performance is often minimal at best. Many of the advancements in golf technology over the years have been incremental, meaning that the gains in performance are marginal and may not be noticeable to the average golfer.

Additionally, golf equipment is highly personal, with each golfer having their own unique swing style and preferences. What works for one golfer may not work for another, and it often takes time and experimentation to find the right equipment that suits your game. Simply buying the latest and greatest equipment without considering your individual needs and preferences is unlikely to lead to better performance.

Moreover, constantly changing your equipment can actually be detrimental to your game, as it can disrupt your consistency and familiarity with your clubs. Golf is a game of repetition and muscle memory, and switching clubs too often can throw off your rhythm and negatively impact your performance.

In conclusion, while it's natural to want to upgrade your golf equipment in hopes of improving your game, it's important to approach this decision with a critical eye. Rather than automatically assuming that new equipment will lead to better performance, consider your individual needs and preferences, and consult with a professional fitter or coach before making any significant changes. Remember, if your current equipment is working well for you, there may be no need to fix what isn't broken.

Word of caution - Beware of Accessories and Training Aids

Golf training aids are devices or tools that are designed to help golfers improve their swing and overall game. While these aids can be helpful in certain situations, it's important to remember that nothing can truly replace the benefits of actually playing the game.

One of the primary advantages of using golf training aids is that they can help golfers identify and correct swing flaws or other issues in their game. For example, a swing trainer can help a golfer improve their swing plane and develop a more consistent swing. Additionally, putting aids can help golfers improve their alignment and develop a more effective putting stroke. Remember, if it sounds too good to be true it probably is.

Using a GPS or rangefinder in golf has become increasingly popular in recent years. These devices allow golfers to accurately measure distances to targets on the course, such as the pin, hazards, or layup points. This information can help golfers make more informed decisions about which club to use and how to approach each shot. Additionally, GPS devices often provide other helpful information such as course layout, hole statistics, and even real-time weather updates. While some purists may argue that relying on technology takes away from the traditional aspect of the game, many golfers find that using a GPS or rangefinder can help them play more confidently and efficiently, ultimately leading to better scores and a more enjoyable round of golf.

However, there are also limitations to using golf training aids. One of the biggest downsides is that they can become a crutch, causing golfers to rely too heavily on the aid rather than developing their own feel and instincts for the game. Additionally, some training aids may not be suitable for all golfers and can actually cause more harm than good.

Perhaps the biggest drawback of relying too heavily on golf training aids is that they can take away from the enjoyment of actually playing the game. Golf is a game of feel and creativity, and constantly focusing on swing mechanics or using aids can detract from the spontaneity and joy of the game.

In conclusion, while golf training aids can be helpful in certain situations, they should not be relied upon as a substitute for actually playing the game. Golfers should focus on developing their own feel and instincts and use aids only when necessary to identify and correct specific issues in their game. Ultimately, the best way to improve as a golfer is to play the game regularly, practice with purpose, and seek guidance from qualified instructors or coaches when needed.

START WITH YOUR GRIP

CHAPTER 5

Critical Step – Check Your Grip

The grip is the foundation of the golf swing and is the first thing that should be mastered by new golfers. A proper grip allows for a solid connection between the golfer and the club, providing greater control and power in the swing. Even after all these years if something isn't working in my swing, I normally start my review with my grip first.

To grip the club properly, start by placing your lead hand (left hand for right-handed golfers, right hand for left-handed golfers) on the grip with your palm facing up. Wrap your fingers around the grip, making sure to keep your thumb pointing down the shaft of the club. Next, place your trail hand (right hand for right-handed golfers, left hand for left-handed golfers) on the grip, with the palm facing down. Wrap your fingers around the grip and place your thumb over the top of your lead hand thumb. The V formed by your thumb and index finger should point towards your trail shoulder.

Understanding the Different Grips in Golf

The grip is one of the most fundamental aspects of a golfer's swing, and it can make all the difference in the accuracy and consistency of your shots. There are three primary grip styles used in golf, each with their unique advantages and disadvantages. In this chapter, we'll take a closer look at each of these grips and discuss their pros and cons.

The Overlapping Grip

The overlapping grip is the most common grip style used in golf. With this grip, you place your little finger of your right hand over the gap between the index finger and middle finger of your left hand. The grip is relatively secure, which makes it perfect for golfers with large hands or those who want to add more control to their swing.

Pros: The overlapping grip is the most natural grip style for most golfers. It's also great for golfers with arthritis or joint problems because it puts less pressure on the hands.

Cons: The overlapping grip can sometimes result in a loss of power or distance because it requires more finesse and less brute force.

The Interlocking Grip

The interlocking grip is similar to the overlapping grip, but instead of placing your little finger over your left index finger, you interlock it with your left index finger. This grip is commonly used by golfers with smaller hands or those who want to generate more power in their swing.

Pros: The interlocking grip is great for golfers who want more power and distance in their shots. It's also a natural grip for those who played sports like baseball or softball.

Cons: The interlocking grip can put extra stress on the joints of the hands, making it a poor choice for golfers with joint issues or arthritis.

The Ten-Finger Grip

The ten-finger grip is also known as the "baseball grip" because it resembles the way you hold a baseball bat. With this grip, you place all ten fingers on the club, creating a unified grip.

Pros: The ten-finger grip is an excellent grip style for beginners, especially children who are just starting with the game. It's also great for golfers who want to add more power and distance to their swing.

Cons: The ten-finger grip can lead to a loss of control because it's more challenging to maintain a consistent grip pressure. It's also not the most natural grip style for most golfers.

In conclusion, choosing the right grip for your game is crucial. The grip you choose should feel comfortable and natural, and it should give you the level of control, power, and accuracy you need for your shots. Experiment with the different grip styles to find the one that works best for you. Remember, the grip is just one aspect of a successful golf swing, so don't forget to work on other aspects of your game, too.

Understanding Weak and Strong Grips in Golf

A golfer's grip is one of the most fundamental components of their swing. The grip is the only point of contact between the golfer and the club, so it has a significant impact on the swing path, clubface angle, and ultimately the ball flight. The grip can be classified as weak or strong, depending on the positioning of the hands on the club. In this chapter, we will discuss what weak and strong grips are, how they affect the swing, and which golfers typically use each type of grip.

What is a Weak Grip?

A weak grip is a grip in which the hands are positioned more towards the left side of the club for right-handed golfers, and more towards the right side for left-handed golfers. This means that the "V" formed by the thumb and index finger of both hands is pointing towards the golfer's chin, rather than towards their right shoulder. With a weak grip, the clubface tends to be more open at impact, resulting in a shot that curves from left to right, also known as a slice.

A weak grip may be suitable for golfers with a natural tendency to hook the ball or who have a very steep swing plane. By adjusting their grip to be weaker, they can counterbalance their tendency to hook the ball and hit more controlled shots with less curvature.

What is a Strong Grip?

A strong grip is a grip in which the hands are positioned more towards the right side of the club for right-handed golfers, and more towards the left side for left-handed golfers. This means that the "V" formed by the thumb and index finger of both hands is pointing towards the golfer's right shoulder, rather than towards their chin. With a strong grip, the clubface tends to be more closed at impact, resulting in a shot that curves from right to left, also known as a hook.

A strong grip may be suitable for golfers who tend to slice the ball or have a shallower swing plane. By adjusting their grip to be stronger, they can counterbalance their tendency to slice the ball and hit more controlled shots with less curvature.

Which Golfers Use Weak and Strong Grips?

Many professional golfers have used weak or strong grips to great effect. For example, Phil Mickelson is known for having a strong grip, while Ben Hogan famously used a weak grip. However, it is important to note that not all golfers will benefit from using either a weak or strong grip.

Beginner golfers are often advised to use a neutral grip, which is when the "V" formed by the thumb and index finger of both hands is pointing towards the centre of the golfer's body. This allows for a more natural swing path and reduces the likelihood of hitting a slice or a hook.

In conclusion, the grip is an essential aspect of the golf swing, and choosing the right grip can significantly impact a golfer's shot shape and consistency. A weak grip can help golfers counteract a natural tendency to hook the ball, while a strong grip can help golfers counteract a natural tendency to slice the ball. However, it is essential to remember that not all golfers will benefit from using a weak or strong grip, and it is essential to experiment and find what works best for each individual golfer.

Critical Step – Position the club in your hands properly

Gripping the club properly is one of the most important aspects of a successful golf swing. A proper grip helps control the clubface, promote accuracy and distance, and reduce the risk of injury. The grip can be broken down into two hands: the lead hand (the left hand for right-handed golfers) and the trail hand (the right hand for right-handed golfers).

The **lead hand should grip the club in the fingers** rather than the palm. This allows for greater control of the clubface and helps promote a proper release through impact. To grip the club correctly with the lead hand, place the club diagonally across the fingers of the left hand, with the grip running from the base of the pinkie finger to the middle joint of the index finger. The thumb should rest slightly to the right of the centre of the grip.

The **trail hand, on the other hand, should grip the club in the palm**. This allows for a more secure grip on the club and promotes greater power through impact. To grip the club correctly with the trail hand, place the club diagonally across the palm of the right hand, with the grip running from the base of the thumb (or as close to the wrist as possible) to the base of the index finger. The thumb should rest slightly to the left of centre.

In addition to the proper grip, it is important to maintain proper hand and wrist alignment throughout the swing. You should **focus on the trail palm facing the target**, this helps to ensure that the clubface remains square at impact, which is crucial for generating power and accuracy. It also promotes a proper release of the club through impact, leading to a more consistent ball flight. Additionally, a properly placed trail hand can help prevent unwanted slices or hooks by minimizing the amount of hand manipulation during the swing. Therefore, it is important for golfers to pay close attention to the position of their trail hand and ensure that it faces the target to achieve the best possible results on the course. **My feel is that the trail palm should point at the target for a neutral shot, to the ground to draw and forward to fade.**

It is essential to have a consistent grip pressure with both hands throughout the swing. A grip that is too tight can restrict the movement of the wrists and arms, while a grip that is too loose can lead to the club slipping and errant shots.

It is also important to note that the grip should be tailored to the individual golfer's hand size, strength, and swing style. A golfer with smaller hands may need to grip the club slightly differently than a golfer with larger hands. Similarly, a golfer who generates a lot of power in their swing may need a firmer grip to control the clubface.

In conclusion, the grip is one of the most important aspects of a successful golf swing. A proper grip allows for greater control of the clubface, promotes accuracy and distance, and reduces the risk of injury. It is important to grip the club correctly with both the lead and trail hand and to maintain proper grip pressure and hand alignment throughout the swing.

Critical Step – Focus on your lead wrist at address

In golf, the position of the lead wrist, which is the left wrist for right-handed golfers, is crucial to the golf swing. At address, it is important not to straighten the lead wrist, as doing so can have negative impacts on the swing.

When the lead wrist is straightened at address, it can cause the clubface to open, meaning the face of the club is pointing away from the target. This can lead to a slice, which is when the ball curves to the right (for right-handed golfers). Additionally, straightening the lead wrist can cause a loss of power, as it limits the amount of wrist hinge in the backswing, which is necessary for generating clubhead speed.

To avoid straightening the lead wrist at address, it is important to maintain a slight bend in the wrist, which is often referred to as a "cupped" position. This position allows the golfer to hinge the wrists during the backswing, creating a wider arc and generating more power in the swing. It also helps to square the clubface at impact, which is necessary for hitting straight shots.

Maintaining a slight bend in the lead wrist at address can be challenging for some golfers, as it may feel unnatural or uncomfortable. However, with practice and repetition, it can become a natural part of the setup routine. Many golfers find it helpful to focus on the feeling of pressure in the fingers and palm of the lead hand to maintain the correct wrist position.

In summary, the lead wrist plays a critical role in the golf swing, and it is important not to straighten it at address. By maintaining a slight bend in the wrist, golfers can generate more power, hit straighter shots, and avoid the slice.

TAKING A STANCE

CHAPTER 6

Building a stable foundation

The stance is another key fundamental of golf technique. A proper stance provides a stable base for the swing and allows for greater control and consistency.

To set up your stance, start by placing your feet shoulder-width apart and positioning the ball in line with your lead foot. Your feet should be parallel to the target line, with your toes pointing slightly outward. Your weight should be distributed evenly between both feet, with slightly more weight on your lead foot.

The stance is a fundamental aspect of golf that has a significant impact on the swing and ball flight. Without a proper stance, it becomes challenging to hit consistent shots and control the ball's direction and distance. This chapter explores the importance of the stance and provides some tips for achieving the right setup.

Balance

One of the primary functions of the stance is to provide balance and stability to the golfer during the swing. A solid base allows for a smoother and more efficient transfer of energy from the body to the clubhead, resulting in better shot-making. The feet should be positioned shoulder-width apart, with the weight evenly distributed on both feet.

Alignment

The stance also influences the alignment of the body to the target. The feet, hips, and shoulders should all be aligned parallel to the target line. Proper alignment allows the golfer to aim accurately and hit the ball on the intended target line.

Ball Position

The position of the ball in relation to the feet is another critical aspect of the stance. The ball's location influences the club's angle of approach, which in turn affects the ball flight. For a driver, the ball should be positioned just inside the left heel, while for shorter irons, the ball should be positioned in the centre of the stance.

Grip Pressure

The stance also affects the golfer's grip pressure, which is crucial for maintaining control over the club throughout the swing. A balanced and stable stance allows for a lighter grip, which helps with generating clubhead speed and releasing the club properly through impact.

Flexibility

The stance should be adapted to suit the golfer's body type and swing style. Golfers with a more upright swing may benefit from a narrower stance, while those with a more rounded swing may require a wider stance for added stability. Additionally, golfers with limited flexibility may need to adjust their stance to allow for a more comfortable and fluid swing.

Practice

Achieving the correct stance takes practice and experimentation. Golfers should spend time on the driving range trying out different stances and noting the results. Recording the swing on video can also help identify any flaws in the setup and address them.

In conclusion, the stance is a crucial component of the golf swing and can significantly impact a golfer's performance. It is essential to achieve a balanced, stable, and comfortable setup to hit consistent shots and control the ball's direction and distance. Practice and experimentation are key to finding the right stance for each golfer's body type and swing style.

Critical Step - Flaring Your Feet

Flaring your feet refers to the positioning of your feet at an angle instead of keeping them parallel to each other. This is a technique that can have a significant impact on your golf swing and the shots you hit, especially for the older players. In this chapter, we will discuss the benefits of flaring your feet and how you can do it properly.

Benefits of Flaring Your Feet:

1. Better Balance: Flaring your feet can help you maintain better balance during your swing. This is because it allows you to shift your weight more easily from one foot to the other. With better balance, you will be able to hit more consistent shots.

2. More Hip Rotation: Flaring your feet can also increase your hip rotation during your swing. This is important because your hips play a crucial role in generating power and clubhead speed. By flaring your feet, you can engage your hips more effectively and hit the ball farther. This is particularly important for older golfers.

3. Better Alignment: Flaring your feet can also help you align yourself properly to the target. This is because it can reduce the chances of you aiming too far left or right. With better alignment, you will be able to hit more accurate shots.

Different ways to Flare Your Feet

1. Open Stance: The most common way to flare your feet is by using an open stance. To do this, position your lead foot (left foot for right-handed golfers and right foot for left-handed golfers) slightly forward and at an angle towards the target. The back foot should be positioned at a slightly smaller angle.

2. Closed Stance: Another way to flare your feet is by using a closed stance. To do this, position your back foot (right foot for right-handed golfers and left foot for left-handed golfers) slightly forward and at an angle towards the target. The front foot should be positioned at a slightly smaller angle.

3. Adjust the Angle: The angle at which you flare your feet will depend on your swing style and personal preference. Experiment with different angles to find what works best for you.

Flaring your feet is a technique that can have a significant impact on your golf swing and the shape of the shots you hit. By increasing your balance, hip rotation, and alignment, you can hit more consistent, powerful, and accurate shots. It is important to experiment with different angles and practice this technique to find what works best for you. Incorporate this technique into your game and see how it can take your golf game to the next level.

Like any other aspect of golf, flaring your feet requires practice. Spend some time on the driving range or practice tee working on your stance and swing with flared feet. Incorporate this technique into your pre-shot routine and see how it affects your game. **This takes time to perfect but can have a significant impact on overall quality of the shot.**

OWN YOUR SWING

CHAPTER 7

No matter what – commit to your swing!

The golf swing is a complex motion that requires a combination of physical and mental skills. A proper swing involves a smooth, fluid motion that generates power and control.

To execute a proper golf swing, start by taking a deep breath and focusing on your target. Begin your backswing by turning your shoulders and hips away from the ball, keeping your arms straight and your wrists firm. At the top of your backswing, pause briefly and check your alignment and positioning. Begin your downswing by turning your hips towards the target and allowing your arms and club to follow through. Contact the ball at the bottom of your swing, striking the ball cleanly and with authority.

Weight distribution plays a crucial role in the golf swing as it can have a significant impact on the power, accuracy, and consistency of your shots. Proper weight distribution throughout the swing will allow you to generate more speed, hit the ball further, and make solid contact more consistently.

The golf swing can be divided into two phases: the backswing and the downswing. During the backswing, weight should be shifted to the back foot to create a stable base and allow for a full shoulder turn. As you begin the downswing, the weight should shift back to the front foot, where it should remain until the follow-through.

In the setup position, your weight should be distributed evenly between your feet. As you begin your backswing, your weight should shift gradually to your back foot, with approximately 60-70% of your weight on your back foot at the top of the backswing. This weight shift is essential to create the necessary coil and torque in the body, which will help generate power and clubhead speed.

During the downswing, all your weight should shift back to your front foot, where it should remain until the follow-through. The weight shift back to the front foot should be smooth and gradual, rather than sudden and jerky. This will allow for a more consistent and powerful strike, as well as a better transfer of energy from the body to the clubhead.

One common mistake that many golfers make is failing to shift their weight properly during the swing. Some golfers may keep too much weight on their front foot, which can cause them to lose power and accuracy. Others may keep too much weight on their back foot, which can cause them to hit the ball fat or thin.

To ensure proper weight distribution in your swing, you should practice with a mirror or video camera to analyse your swing. Look for any major weight shifts or imbalances, and work on adjusting as needed. You may also want to work with a golf instructor, who can provide feedback and guidance on proper weight distribution and other aspects of your swing.

In conclusion, weight distribution is a crucial element of the golf swing. Proper weight distribution will help you generate more power, accuracy, and consistency in your shots. By practicing proper weight distribution and working with a qualified instructor, you can improve your swing and become a more effective golfer.

Different Paths of Golf Swing

The golf swing is a complex motion that involves a sequence of movements to produce the desired ball flight. One of the most critical aspects of the golf swing is the path that the clubhead follows during the swing. The swing path can significantly impact the ball's direction, spin, and launch angle. In this chapter, we'll discuss the different paths of the golf swing and how they can affect your shots.

The Inside-Out Path

The inside-out path is one of the most common swing paths for players who want to hit a draw shot. The clubhead starts inside the target line on the downswing and then moves out towards the ball's right, creating an in-to-out swing path. This type of swing path creates a right-to-left spin on the ball, resulting in a draw shot. To achieve an inside-out path, players must focus on keeping their hands and arms closer to their body on the downswing while maintaining proper hip rotation.

The Outside-In Path

The outside-in swing path is the opposite of the inside-out path. The clubhead moves outside the target line on the downswing and then comes back inside towards the ball's left, creating an out-to-in swing path. This type of swing path results in a left-to-right spin on the ball, resulting in a slice shot. Players who struggle with an outside-in path often have a steep downswing and an early release, causing the clubhead to come over the top.

The Straight Path

The straight path is the ideal swing path for most shots, especially when playing straight or fade shots. The clubhead moves straight down the target line on the downswing and then continues along the same path through impact. This type of swing path produces a minimal spin on the ball, resulting in a straight or slight fade shot. To achieve a straight path, players must focus on maintaining a neutral wrist position, proper weight transfer, and a consistent swing plane.

The Square-to-Square Path

The square-to-square swing path is a popular technique used by many golfers, including Jim Furyk and Matt Kuchar. This type of swing path involves taking the club back straight and then bringing it down the same path to impact, creating a square-to-square motion. This swing path promotes a consistent ball flight and helps eliminate big misses to the left or right. To achieve a square-to-square path, players must focus on a short backswing, proper weight transfer, and a stable lower body.

Search for feedback

The swing path is an essential aspect of the golf swing that can significantly impact your shots. The inside-out, outside-in, straight, and square-to-square paths are the most common paths used by golfers. Each swing path has its unique characteristics and requires specific swing mechanics to execute successfully. By understanding the different paths of the golf swing, players can make better swing decisions and produce more consistent shots.

Using Video Analysis One of the most effective tools for improving your golf technique is video analysis. By recording your swing and reviewing it with an instructor, you can identify areas for improvement and adjust your technique. Using video analysis can help you identify flaws in your grip, stance, and swing, and provide targeted feedback on how to improve.

Mastering the fundamentals of golf technique is essential to success on the course. In this chapter, we covered the proper grip, stance, and swing, as well as the benefits of using video analysis to identify areas for improvement. By mastering these fundamentals and working with an experienced instructor, you can improve your performance and take your game to the next level. In the next chapter, we will explore the importance of course management and how to develop a winning strategy for the course.

Critical Step - The Importance of a Smooth Swing

Golf is a game of finesse and skill, requiring a combination of physical and mental prowess. One of the fundamental elements of the game is the swing, which is often considered the foundation of good golf. A smooth swing is crucial to playing consistently well, and it is an attribute that golfers of all levels aspire to achieve.

What is a smooth swing?

A smooth swing is characterized by a fluid, rhythmic motion that allows the clubhead to accelerate through the ball. It is often associated with a sense of effortlessness, as if the golfer is effortlessly sweeping the club through the ball with ease. In contrast, a jerky or awkward swing can result in mishits, inconsistency, and frustration.

Why is a smooth swing important?

There are several reasons why a smooth swing is essential in golf. Firstly, it helps to generate clubhead speed, which is a critical factor in hitting the ball long distances. When the swing is smooth, the clubhead accelerates smoothly through the ball, maximizing the transfer of energy from the club to the ball. This generates more ball speed, leading to longer shots.

Secondly, a smooth swing promotes consistency. When the swing is smooth, the golfer is more likely to make solid contact with the ball, resulting in more accurate shots. Inconsistent swings, on the other hand, can result in mishits, slices, and hooks, leading to errant shots and higher scores.

Finally, a smooth swing can help to reduce tension and stress on the golfer's body. When the swing is jerky or forced, it can lead to muscle strain, tension, and even injury. A smooth swing allows the golfer to maintain a relaxed and natural posture, reducing the risk of injury and promoting longevity in the game.

How to achieve a smooth swing?

Achieving a smooth swing requires practice, patience, and a commitment to technique. Some tips to help achieve a smooth swing include:

1. Focus on tempo: A smooth swing is all about rhythm and timing. Practice swinging the club at a consistent tempo, with a smooth and fluid motion.

2. Keep your grip relaxed: A tight grip can lead to tension in the arms and shoulders, resulting in a jerky swing. Keep your grip relaxed and natural, allowing for a smooth and fluid motion.

3. Stay balanced: A smooth swing requires good balance and stability. Practice maintaining a solid base throughout the swing, with your weight evenly distributed.

4. Use your body: A smooth swing involves using your entire body, not just your arms and hands. Practice engaging your core and hips to create a smooth and fluid motion.

5. Practice, practice, practice: Achieving a smooth swing requires consistent practice and repetition. Take the time to work on your swing, both on the range and on the course.

In conclusion, a smooth swing is crucial to playing good golf. It helps to generate power and consistency, reduces the risk of injury, and promotes a sense of relaxation and ease on the course. By focusing on technique and committing to practice, any golfer can achieve a smooth swing and enjoy the benefits it brings to their game.

Critical Step – Maintain width in the swing

Width in a golf swing refers to the amount of extension and separation between the arms and the body during the backswing and downswing. It is an important element in achieving a powerful and consistent golf swing.

During the backswing, maintaining width allows the golfer to create a wider arc and generate more power. This is because the extension between the arms and body creates a greater lever, allowing for a larger, more powerful turn. Conversely, if the golfer collapses their arms or brings them too close to the body, the arc becomes smaller, and the power and accuracy of the swing can suffer.

In the downswing, width helps the golfer maintain the proper swing plane and sequence, preventing the club from getting too far behind or in front of the body. This allows for a more consistent ball flight and greater control over the shot.

To achieve and maintain width, golfers should focus on keeping their lead arm straight and their trail arm slightly bent throughout the swing. The lead arm should function as a guide, while the trail arm provides support and stability. The hands should be positioned in front of the chest, and the shoulders should rotate around the spine, allowing the arms to maintain their extension.

Maintaining width requires a combination of flexibility, strength, and technique, and it may take some time and practice to achieve. However, once mastered, it can be a game-changer in terms of power, consistency, and accuracy in a golfer's swing.

PUTTING

CHAPTER 8

Introduction to putting

Putting can either make or break your game. Even the most skilled golfers struggle with their putting from time to time. But don't worry, with the right mindset, techniques, and practices, you can become a pro at putting.

Putting is the act of rolling the ball into the hole using a putter. The goal of putting is to get the ball into the hole in as few strokes as possible. To do this, you need to have a good grip, stance, and swing.

Putting is important because it accounts for more than 40% of your total score. Even if you hit the ball well on the fairway, it doesn't matter if you can't putt. Putting can make or break your game, so it's crucial to focus on improving your putting skills.

Putting is not just a physical skill; it's also a mental game. You need to be confident and have a positive mindset when you're putting. Visualization is an essential technique that can help you imagine the ball going into the hole, which can boost your confidence and help you focus on your target.

Even the best golfers make mistakes when putting. Common mistakes include improper grip, poor alignment, and lack of focus. By identifying and correcting these mistakes, you can improve your putting game and become a better golfer.

There are many putting drills that you can do to improve your putting skills. One drill is to practice your distance control by placing markers at different distances and trying to land the ball on them. Another drill is to practice your aim by putting a towel down and trying to land the ball on it.

Here are some putting tips to help you improve your game:

- Keep your head still and your eyes on the ball.
- The back of the lead hand and the palm of the trail hand should face the target.
- Use a light grip to maintain control and feel.
- Focus on your target and visualize the ball going into the hole.
- Practice regularly to improve your skills.

Putting is a crucial part of golf, and improving your putting skills can make a big difference in your game. By focusing on the basics, mental preparation, techniques, and practices, you can become a pro at putting. With dedication and practice, you'll be sinking putts like a pro in no time!

Putting is perhaps the most important aspect of the short game. It's the shot that's taken on every hole and can account for over 40% of your shots during a round. In this chapter, we'll cover the fundamentals of putting, as well as some tips and practice drills to help you improve your putting skills. By mastering the fundamentals of putting, learning how to read greens, and practicing regularly, you'll be able to shave strokes off your score and become a more confident and consistent putter.

The importance of putting

Putting is often referred to as the "scoring zone" of golf because it's where the majority of your shots are taken. A skilled putter can make up for a lot of mistakes made on the fairway and still have a good score. On the other hand, even a great ball striker can struggle to score well if they can't putt.

One of the reasons putting is so important is that it requires a different skillset than the rest of the game. Driving and iron shots require power and accuracy, while putting requires finesse and touch. It's not enough to just hit the ball in the right direction; you need to judge the speed, break, and slope of the green to sink the putt.

Another reason putting is so crucial is that it can be a great equalizer in golf. A high-handicap golfer may struggle off the tee and with their iron shots, but if they can putt well, they can still score low. Conversely, a low-handicap golfer may hit the ball well but struggle with their putting, resulting in a high score.

The importance of putting is reflected in the scoring system of golf. Each hole is assigned a par, which is the number of strokes a skilled golfer should be able to complete the hole in. Par is calculated based on the distance and difficulty of the hole. The fewer strokes it takes to complete a hole, the lower the score. Putting is where you can make up strokes and score well.

In summary, putting is important because it requires a different skillset than the rest of the game, can be a great equalizer, and is reflected in the scoring system of golf. In the next chapter, we'll talk about the mental preparation required for successful putting.

Different Putting Grips

The grip you use when putting can have a significant impact on your ability to control the ball's speed and direction. There are several different putting grips to choose from, and in this chapter, we'll explore some of the most popular options.

1. Standard grip: The standard grip is the most common grip used by golfers when putting. It involves placing both hands on the putter grip, with the thumbs pointing down the shaft. The standard grip is a good option for beginners and those looking for a simple, straightforward approach to putting.

2. Cross-handed grip: The cross-handed grip involves placing your lead hand (the hand closest to the hole) below your trail hand (the hand furthest from the hole). This grip can help to eliminate wrist movement and provide more stability in the putting stroke.

3. Claw grip: The claw grip involves placing the trail hand on the grip in a "claw" position, with the fingers pointing down towards the ground. This grip can help to reduce wrist movement and promote a more stable stroke.

4. Left-hand low grip: The left-hand low grip involves placing your lead hand below your trail hand, with your lead hand gripping the putter lower on the grip than your trail hand. This grip can help to promote a smoother, more consistent stroke.

5. Split-handed grip: The split-handed grip involves placing the hands on the grip with a gap between them. The trail hand is placed lower on the grip than the lead hand. This grip can help to promote a more relaxed grip pressure and provide more control over the putter face.

6. Arm-lock grip: The arm-lock grip involves locking the lead arm against your side and gripping the putter with the trail hand. This grip can help to promote a more stable stroke and provide more control over the putter face.

In summary, there are several different putting grips to choose from, each with its own advantages and disadvantages. The standard grip, cross-handed grip, claw grip, left-hand low grip, split-handed grip, and arm-lock grip are some of the most popular options. By experimenting with different grips, you can find the one that works best for your putting style and helps you achieve your goals on the greens.

Reading Greens

Reading the green is a crucial skill when it comes to putting. Knowing how to read the slope, break, and speed of the green can make a big difference in your putting game. In this chapter, we'll explore some tips to help you improve your ability to read greens.

1. Observe the green from all angles: Before you approach the green, take the time to observe it from all angles. Walk around the green and take note of any slope or contours that could affect your putt.

2. Look for high points and low points: Look for high points and low points on the green, as these can help you identify the slope and break of the green. The ball will break towards the low points and away from the high points.

3. Check the grain of the grass: The grain of the grass can affect the speed and direction of your putt. Make sure you take the time to check the grain of the grass, as this can help you determine the speed and direction of the putt.

4. Use your putter as a level: Your putter can be a useful tool for determining the slope of the green. Place your putter flat on the green and observe the angle. This can help you determine the slope and break of the green.

5. Consider the speed of the green: The speed of the green can also affect your putting game. Take note of how fast or slow the green is running and adjust your putt accordingly.

6. Look for subtle breaks: Sometimes the break of the green can be subtle, so it's important to pay close attention to the green as you approach it. Look for any subtle breaks that could affect the direction of your putt.

7. Trust your instincts: Reading greens can be a challenging skill, and it's important to trust your instincts when making a decision about your putt. If you feel confident about the line and speed of your putt, trust your instincts and go for it.

In summary, reading greens is an essential skill for any golfer looking to improve their putting game. By observing the green from all angles, looking for high and low points, checking the grain of the grass, using your putter as a level, considering the speed of the green, looking for subtle breaks, and trusting your instincts, you can become a more skilled and confident green reader.

Common Putting Mistakes to Avoid

Even the best golfers make mistakes on the greens. In this chapter, we'll explore some common putting mistakes to avoid.

1. Lack of focus: Lack of focus is one of the most common mistakes made on the greens. If you're not fully focused on your putt, you're more likely to miss it. Develop a pre-shot routine and stick to it every time you putt to help you stay focused and consistent.

2. Poor alignment: Poor alignment is another common putting mistake. Make sure that your putter is aligned with the ball and the target line, and that your feet and shoulders are aligned as well. This helps to ensure that your stroke is on the correct line.

3. Hitting the ball too hard: Hitting the ball too hard is a common mistake, especially when putting uphill. Focus on speed control and hit the ball with just enough force to reach the hole.

4. Not reading the green: Failing to read the green is a major mistake when it comes to putting. Take your time to analyse the slope and break of the green and consider how it will affect the roll of the ball. Use your putter to gauge the speed of the green and adjust your stroke accordingly.

5. Gripping the putter too tightly: Gripping the putter too tightly can affect your stroke and lead to inconsistent putting. Hold the putter with a relaxed grip and use your shoulders and arms to control the stroke.

6. Rushing the stroke: Rushing the stroke is another common mistake that can lead to missed putts. Take your time and focus on your pre-shot routine to help you stay relaxed and consistent.

In summary, common putting mistakes to avoid include lack of focus, poor alignment, hitting the ball too hard, not reading the green, gripping the putter too tightly, and rushing the stroke. By avoiding these mistakes and focusing on improving your technique and mental game, you can become a more skilled and confident putter.

Routine & Tips

Improving your putting is a key component to lowering your golf scores. In this chapter, we'll explore some tips and strategies to help you improve your putting game.

1. Practice, practice, practice: The best way to improve your putting is through consistent practice. Set aside time to work on your putting stroke and focus on improving your technique and accuracy. Use putting drills, such as the gate drill or the ladder drill, to help you hone your skills.

2. Develop a pre-shot routine: A pre-shot routine helps you to stay focused and consistent when putting. Develop a routine that works for you, such as taking a deep breath, lining up your putt, and taking a practice swing. Stick to this routine every time you putt to build consistency and confidence.

3. Read the green: Reading the green is a crucial aspect of successful putting. Take your time to analyse the slope and break of the green and consider how it will affect the roll of the ball. Use your putter to gauge the speed of the green and adjust your stroke accordingly.

4. Use the right putter: The type of putter you use can affect your performance on the greens. Experiment with different types of putters, such as blade putters or mallet putters, to find the one that works best for you. Also, make sure that your putter is the correct length and has the right amount of loft for your stroke.

5. Focus on speed control: Controlling the speed of your putt is just as important as the direction. Practice hitting putts with different levels of speed to get a feel for the greens. If you consistently hit putts too hard or too soft, adjust your stroke accordingly.

6. Visualize the putt: Visualization is a powerful tool when it comes to putting. Before you hit your putt, visualize the ball sinking into the hole. This helps to build confidence and focus and can improve your overall performance on the greens.

In summary, improving your putting game requires consistent practice, a pre-shot routine, reading the green, using the right putter, focusing on speed control, and visualizing the putt. By incorporating these tips into your practice routine, you can become a more skilled and confident putter.

Critical Step - The Mental Game of Putting

Putting is not just a physical act; it's also a mental one. Successful putting requires focus, confidence, and the ability to stay calm under pressure. In this chapter, we'll explore the mental preparation required for successful putting.

First and foremost, you need to have a positive mindset when putting. Confidence in your abilities is crucial. If you approach a putt with doubt or fear, you're more likely to miss it. On the other hand, if you approach a putt with confidence and belief in your abilities, you're more likely to make it. Visualize the ball sinking into the hole and focus on the successful outcome.

Secondly, you need to be able to read the green and judge the speed and break of the putt. This requires focus and diligence. Take your time to analyse the slope and grain of the green and consider how it will affect the roll of the ball. Practice your pre-shot routine to help you stay focused and consistent.

Another key aspect of the mental game of putting is managing your emotions. It's easy to get frustrated or angry when you miss a putt, but this will only make it harder to succeed on the next one. Learn to let go of mistakes and stay calm under pressure. Remember that every putt is an opportunity to improve your score, regardless of the outcome of the earlier one.

Finally, it's important to practice putting under pressure. This can mean playing in competitive situations or setting up drills that simulate the pressure of a real game. The more you practice putting under pressure, the better prepared you'll be to handle it in a real game.

In summary, successful putting requires a positive mindset, focus, attention to detail, and the ability to manage your emotions and practice under pressure. By honing your mental game, you can improve your putting and your overall golf game.

Critical Step - Putting from Off the Green

Putting from off the green, also known as "chipping with a putter," can be a useful technique for getting the ball close to the hole and saving strokes. In this chapter, we'll explore some tips for putting from off the green.

1. Assess the lie: Before trying a putt from off the green, assess the lie of the ball. Is the ball sitting up or nestled in the grass? Is the grass long or short? The lie will affect the amount of power and loft you need to use.

2. Choose the right putter: Not all putters are created equal when it comes to putting from off the green. Choose a putter with a bit of loft, such as a hybrid putter, to help get the ball in the air and rolling towards the hole.

3. Use a pendulum stroke: When putting from off the green, use a pendulum stroke that is similar to your regular putting stroke. Keep your wrists firm and use your shoulders to create a smooth, consistent motion.

4. Aim for the fringe: When putting from off the green, aim for the fringe around the green instead of the hole. This will help you avoid any bumps or undulations that could cause the ball to veer off course.

5. Use the slope: When putting from off the green, use the slope of the green to your advantage. Aim for a spot on the green where the slope will naturally carry the ball towards the hole.

6. Practice, practice, practice: Putting from off the green is a skill that takes practice to master. Spend some time on the practice green working on your technique and experimenting with different putters and strategies.

In summary, putting from off the green can be a useful technique for getting the ball close to the hole and saving strokes. To successfully putt from off the green, assess the lie of the ball, choose the right putter, use a pendulum stroke, aim for the fringe, use the slope, and practice regularly. With these tips, you'll be able to putt from confidently and successfully off the green.

THE SHORT GAME

CHAPTER 9

Introduction to the Short Game

Golf is often referred to as a game of precision, and nowhere is precision more important than in the short game. While the long game may get all the attention, it's the short game that separates the good players from the great players. The short game refers to shots played from within 100 yards of the green, and it includes putting, chipping, pitching, and bunker play.

In this chapter, we'll provide an overview of the short game and its importance in golf. We'll also cover some basic short game techniques that will help you get started on improving your game.

Overview of the Short Game The short game is often considered the most important part of golf, as it accounts for a significant percentage of shots played during a round. A great short game can make up for deficiencies in other areas of your game, while a poor short game can prevent you from scoring well even if you hit long shots well.

The four main components of the short game are chipping, pitching, lobbing and bunker play. Each of these requires different techniques and skills, but they all have one thing in common: precision.

Importance of Developing a Good Short Game Developing a good short game is critical if you want to improve your scores and become a better golfer. A strong short game will allow you to save strokes by getting up and down from around the green, while a weak short game will result in wasted shots and higher scores.

A good short game also supplies a mental advantage, as you'll be more confident and relaxed knowing that you have the skills to save par or even make birdie from difficult positions.

Basic Short Game Techniques The techniques used in the short game are different from those used in the long game, as they need more finesse and precision. Some basic short game techniques include:

- Gripping the club lightly to maintain control and feel

- Keeping your weight on the front foot for stability and control

- Keeping your head still and your eyes on the ball

- Using a shallow, descending angle of attack for chipping and pitching

- Using the bounce of the club to control spin

In the following chapters, we'll delve deeper into each aspect of the short game, providing detailed instruction and tips for improvement. By mastering these techniques and practicing regularly, you'll develop a strong short game that will help you lower your scores and enjoy the game of golf even more.

Pitching

Pitching is a crucial aspect of the short game that can help you get the ball close to the hole from a variety of distances around the green. In this chapter, we'll cover the basics of pitching, different types of pitch shots, and some practice drills to help you improve your pitching skills.

Fundamentals of Pitching requires a slightly longer backswing than chipping, as well as a more aggressive follow-through. Here are some fundamental techniques to keep in mind when pitching:

- Use a slightly wider stance than chipping, with your weight on the front foot

- Grip the club lightly, with your hands slightly ahead of the ball

- Take a longer backswing than chipping, and accelerate through the ball for more power

- Keep your head steady and your eyes on the ball

- Aim for a spot on the green where you want the ball to land

Types of Pitch Shots There are several types of pitch shots that you can use depending on the distance and the situation. Here are some common types of pitch shots:

- Basic Pitch: A basic pitch shot is a low, running shot that rolls out towards the hole

- High Pitch: A high pitch shot is a lofted shot that lands softly on the green and stops quickly

- Spin Pitch: A spin pitch shot is a high, lofted shot that generates backspin and stops quickly on the green

- Bump-and-Run Pitch: A bump-and-run pitch shot is a low, running shot that bounces once on the green and rolls out towards the hole

Practice Drills for Improving Pitching Practicing regularly is key to improving your pitching skills. Here are some drills to help you develop better control, accuracy, and feel:

- Distance Control Drill: Set up several balls at different distances from the hole and try to pitch each ball to land within a small circle around the hole.

- Up-and-Down Drill: Hit a pitch shot from off the green, and then try to make the putt from where the ball lands.

- Pitching to a Target Drill: Set up a target on the green (such as a bucket or a hoop), and practice pitching to hit the target.

By mastering the fundamentals of pitching, learning the different types of pitch shots, and practicing regularly, you'll be able to get the ball closer to the hole from a variety of distances and save strokes on your scorecard.

Chipping

Chipping is another critical aspect of the short game that can save you strokes around the green. In this chapter, we'll cover the fundamentals of chipping, as well as some tips and practice drills to help you improve your chipping skills.

Fundamentals of Chipping

Chipping is all about control and accuracy. Here are some fundamentals to keep in mind when chipping:

- Use a narrow stance with the ball positioned towards the back foot

- Grip the club lightly with your hands ahead of the ball

- Keep your wrists firm during the stroke

- Use a short backswing and follow-through

- Accelerate through the ball for a crisp contact

- Aim for a spot on the green where you want the ball to land

Types of Chipping Shots

There are several types of chipping shots that you can use depending on the situation. Here are some common types of chipping shots:

- Basic Chip: A basic chip shot is a low, running shot that rolls out towards the hole

- Flop Shot: A flop shot is a high, soft shot that lands on the green and stops quickly

- Bump-and-Run: A bump-and-run is a low, running shot that bounces once on the green and rolls out towards the hole

- Lob Shot: A lob shot is a high, soft shot that lands on the green and stops quickly, but with more spin than a flop shot

Practice Drills for Improving

Chipping Practicing regularly is key to improving your chipping skills. Here are some drills to help you develop better control, accuracy, and feel:

- Circle Drill: Set up several balls around the hole and chip each ball towards the hole. Try to get each ball to stop within a small circle around the hole.

- Three Club Drill: Practice chipping with three different clubs (e.g., sand wedge, pitching wedge, 8-iron) to develop better feel and control.

- Up-and-Down Drill: Hit a chip shot from off the green, and then try to make the putt from where the ball lands.

By mastering the fundamentals of chipping, learning the different types of chipping shots, and practicing regularly, you'll be able to get up and down from around the green more often and save strokes on your scorecard.

Sand Shots

Getting out of a bunker can be a daunting task for many golfers, but with some basic techniques and practice, you can become more comfortable with this aspect of the short game. In this chapter, we'll cover the basics of sand shots, including setup, swing mechanics, and some practice drills to help you improve your sand play.

Setup for Sand Shots The setup for a sand shot is different from other shots in the short game. Here are the key points to keep in mind when setting up for a sand shot:

- Open the clubface to add loft to the shot

- Dig your feet into the sand to create a stable base

- Position the ball forward in your stance

- Aim to hit behind the ball and splash the sand out of the bunker

Swing Mechanics for Sand Shots The swing for a sand shot is similar to a normal full swing, but with a few key differences. Here's how to execute a sand shot:

- Take a slightly longer backswing than a normal shot, and accelerate through the ball

- Aim to hit the sand about an inch behind the ball

- Keep your head steady and your eyes on the ball throughout the shot

- Allow the club to slide through the sand, rather than trying to lift the ball out of the bunker

Practice Drills for Sand Shots Practicing your sand shots can help you build confidence and improve your ability to get out of bunkers. Here are some drills to help you develop better technique and control:

- Bunker Shots to Different Targets Drill: Set up several targets around the bunker and practice hitting shots to each target from different positions in the bunker.

- Bunker Play with One Club Drill: Use a single club (such as a sand wedge) to practice hitting a variety of different sand shots from different lies in the bunker.

- Buried Lie in the Bunker Drill: Practice hitting shots from a buried lie in the bunker by placing the ball in a deep depression in the sand.

By mastering the setup and swing mechanics for sand shots, and practicing regularly, you can become more comfortable and confident with your ability to get out of bunkers and save strokes on your scorecard.

Specialty Shots

While the majority of shots in golf are played from a level lie, there will be times when you encounter uneven lies or situations that require you to hit a specialty shot. In this chapter, we'll cover some of the most common specialty shots you may encounter on the course, and give you tips on how to execute them successfully.

Chip-and-Run

The chip-and-run shot is a low trajectory shot that is ideal for when you need to get the ball rolling quickly along the ground. Here's how to execute a good chip-and-run shot:

- Use a club with less loft, such as a 7-iron or 8-iron

- Position the ball in the middle of your stance

- Keep your weight on your front foot throughout the shot

- Make a simple, abbreviated swing with a firm wrist

Flop Shot

The flop shot is a high, soft shot that is used when you need to carry the ball over an obstacle and stop it quickly on the green. Here's how to execute a good flop shot:

- Use a club with more loft, such as a sand wedge or lob wedge

- Position the ball forward in your stance

- Open the clubface to add loft to the shot

- Make a full, high swing with a lot of wrist hinge

Punch Shot

The punch shot is a low, penetrating shot that is used when you need to keep the ball under the wind or when you have an obstacle in your path. Here's how to execute a good punch shot:

- Use a club with less loft, such as a 3-iron or 4-iron

- Position the ball back in your stance

- Keep your weight on your front foot throughout the shot

- Make a shorter, more compact swing with a firm wrist

Bunker Shot from a Buried Lie

A bunker shot from a buried lie is one of the most difficult shots in golf. Here's how to execute a good bunker shot from a buried lie:

- Use a sand wedge or lob wedge with a sharp leading edge

- Position the ball forward in your stance

- Maintain a neutral clubface

- Dig your feet in deeply to create a stable base

- Make a steep, aggressive swing, hitting the sand behind the ball

In conclusion, mastering these advanced short game techniques will allow you to take your game to the next level and become a more versatile and skilled golfer. Practice these shots on the range and incorporate them into your game to see a noticeable improvement in your short game performance.

Critical Step - The Importance of Wrist Angles with Wedges

When it comes to hitting wedge shots, one of the most important factors to consider is wrist angles. Proper wrist angles can help you achieve better control over the ball flight, spin, and trajectory of your shots. In this chapter, we'll discuss the importance of wrist angles with wedges and how to achieve the correct ones.

The Importance of Using the Bounce on Your Wedges

When it comes to hitting wedge shots around the green, many golfers focus solely on the loft of the club. However, the bounce of the wedge is just as important, if not more so, in producing clean and effective shots.

The bounce of a wedge refers to the angle between the leading edge and the trailing edge of the clubhead. A high bounce angle means there is more space between the leading edge and the ground, which can help prevent the club from digging into the turf and producing a chunked shot. On the other hand, a low bounce angle means there is less space between the leading edge and the ground, which can lead to the club digging in too much and producing a thin shot.

Using the bounce effectively can help you produce crisp, clean shots with your wedges. Here are some tips for using the bounce:

- Open the clubface: When hitting a wedge shot, try opening the clubface slightly to increase the bounce angle. This will help prevent the club from digging in too much and produce a shallower angle of attack.
- Use a shallow swing: When hitting a wedge shot, try to swing the club more shallowly, with less of a descending angle of attack. This will help the club glide along the turf and make more use of the bounce.
- Hit down and through the ball: While using the bounce is important, it's still important to hit down and through the ball to produce the necessary spin and height on your shots. Focus on striking the ball first and then allowing the bounce to come into play.
- Practice with different bounce angles: Different wedges will have different bounce angles, so it's important to practice with different clubs and angles to find what works best for you in different situations.

In conclusion, using the bounce on your wedges is a key part of producing clean and effective shots around the green. By understanding the bounce angle of your clubs and using it effectively, you can produce more consistent and accurate wedge shots. Practice using the bounce in different situations to find what works best for you and remember to focus on hitting down and through the ball while allowing the bounce to do its job.

What Are Wrist Angles?
Wrist angles refer to the position of your wrists in relation to the clubface at impact. There are two types of wrist angles: dorsiflexion and palmar flexion. Dorsiflexion is when the top of your wrist is bent back towards your forearm, while palmar flexion is when the top of your wrist is bent forward towards your palm.

Why Are Wrist Angles Important with Wedges?
Wrist angles are particularly important when hitting wedge shots because they can help you achieve the right amount of spin and trajectory on the ball. The proper wrist angles will also help you control the distance and direction of your shots.

When hitting wedge shots, you want to have a slightly open clubface and maintain the angle throughout the swing. Having the correct wrist angles will help you achieve this. If your wrists are too open or too closed, it will affect the clubface angle and cause the ball to go off target.

How to Achieve the Correct Wrist Angles
To achieve the correct wrist angles with your wedges, you need to maintain a firm grip on the club and keep your hands ahead of the ball at impact. This will help you achieve a downward strike on the ball, which is crucial for generating spin and controlling distance.

As you swing through the ball, try to maintain the same wrist angles you had at address. This will help you maintain a consistent ball flight and trajectory. If you're struggling to achieve the correct wrist angles, try hitting some half shots and focusing on maintaining the correct wrist position throughout the swing.

Wrist angles are an important factor to consider when hitting wedge shots. They can help you achieve the right amount of spin and trajectory on the ball, which is crucial for controlling distance and direction. To achieve the correct wrist angles, maintain a firm grip on the club and keep your hands ahead of the ball at impact. Practice hitting half shots and focus on maintaining the correct wrist position throughout the swing. With practice, you'll be able to achieve the correct wrist angles and hit more accurate and consistent wedge shots.

Critical Step - Possible grip change in short game

In golf, the grip is one of the most essential aspects of the swing. Having the proper grip can greatly impact the outcome of the shot. This is especially true for the short game, where precision and touch are critical. There are several different grips that golfers can use when playing their short game shots, and each has its own benefits and drawbacks. In this chapter, we will take a closer look at some of the different grips used in the short game.

1. The Standard Grip The standard grip is the most commonly used grip in golf. It involves placing your hands on the club in a neutral position, with your palms facing each other. This grip is easy to learn and is suitable for most shots, including the short game. However, the standard grip does not offer as much control as some of the other grips and may not be suitable for golfers who require a more aggressive shot.

2. The Reverse Overlap Grip The reverse overlap grip is a popular grip for golfers who want more control over their shots. This grip involves placing the little finger of your right hand over the index finger of your left hand. The reverse overlap grip is especially useful for short game shots, where control and touch are critical.

When it comes to the short game, selecting the right grip is crucial. A good grip will allow you to have better control and touch on the ball, resulting in more accurate shots. Golfers should experiment with different grips to see which one works best for their playing style and technique. By mastering the proper grip, golfers can improve their short game and overall performance on the course.

Short Game Strategies

A great short game requires more than just technical skill. To consistently score low on the course, you need to have a solid strategy for approaching each shot around the green. In this chapter, we'll discuss some effective short game strategies to help you make the most of your skills.

1. Assessing the Lie Before you even step up to your shot, you need to assess the lie of the ball. Look at the grass and ground around the ball to determine if it's sitting up, buried in the rough, or on an upslope or downslope. The lie will determine what type of shot you can execute and what club to use.

2. Choosing the Right Club Once you've assessed the lie, you need to choose the right club for the shot. Different shots require different clubs, and it's important to choose the right one to execute the shot effectively.

For example, a bump and run shot requires a pitching or gap wedge, while a flop shot requires a lob wedge.

3. Visualizing the Shot Before you execute the shot, take a moment to visualize the shot in your mind. Imagine the trajectory of the ball, the height and distance it will travel, and where it will land on the green. This mental preparation will help you execute the shot with confidence and precision.

4. Reading the Green Reading the green is just as important as assessing the lie and choosing the right club. Look at the slope and contour of the green to determine how the ball will roll once it lands. Take note of any breaks or undulations in the green that may affect the ball's path.

5. Adjusting for Wind and Weather Wind and weather conditions can have a significant impact on short game shots. Adjust your shot and club selection accordingly. For example, if there's a strong headwind, you may need to use a more lofted club or adjust your trajectory to compensate for the wind.

6. Practicing Different Scenarios To improve your short game strategy, practice different scenarios on the practice range or putting green. Practice uphill, downhill, and sidehill lies, and practice shots from different distances and angles. The more you practice, the better you'll be able to assess each shot and make the right decisions on the course.

By incorporating these short game strategies into your game, you'll be able to approach each shot with a clear plan and execute it with confidence and precision. Remember to assess the lie, choose the right club, visualize the shot, read the green, adjust for wind and weather, and practice different scenarios to become a more skilled and strategic short game player.

Mental Game of the Short Game

Golf is a game that requires both physical and mental skills. While the physical skills are important, the mental aspect of the game can often be the difference between success and failure, especially when it comes to the short game. In this chapter, we'll cover some of the key mental skills that you can develop to improve your short game performance.

Focus

One of the most important mental skills in golf is focus. When playing short game shots, it's essential to focus on the task at hand and block out any distractions. Here are some tips to help you improve your focus:

- Visualize the shot in your mind before hitting it

- Take a deep breath and clear your mind before each shot

- Stay in the moment and avoid thinking about past or future shots

- Use positive self-talk to stay confident and focused

Confidence

Confidence is another crucial mental skill in golf. When you're confident in your short game, you'll be more likely to execute your shots successfully. Here are some tips to help you build confidence in your short game:

- Practice your short game regularly to build your skills and familiarity

- Focus on your strengths and play to them

- Use positive self-talk to reinforce your confidence

- Set realistic goals and celebrate your successes

Patience

Patience is a virtue in golf, especially when it comes to the short game. Short game shots require precision and finesse, which can take time to master. Here are some tips to help you cultivate patience in your short game:

- Practice regularly and be patient with your progress

- Accept that mistakes will happen and focus on the next shot

- Stay calm and composed, even under pressure

- Stay in the present moment and avoid getting ahead of yourself

In conclusion, the mental aspect of the short game can be just as important as the physical skills. By developing your focus, confidence, and patience, you can improve your short game performance and become a more successful golfer.

LONG & APPROACH SHOTS

CHAPTER 10

Importance of Approach Shots

Golf is a game of precision, and no shot requires more precision than an approach shot. Approach shots refer to the shots played from the fairway or rough onto the green. These shots can range from short wedge shots to longer iron shots and are crucial to scoring well in golf.

Many golfers spend a lot of time working on their driving and putting, but approach shots are often overlooked. However, approach shots are critical to setting up birdie opportunities and avoiding bogeys. In fact, according to statistics from the PGA Tour, approach shots account for over 50% of scoring opportunities for the pros.

One of the reasons why approach shots are so important is that they require accuracy and distance control. A slight miss-hit on an approach shot can result in a shot that is short or long of the green, leaving a difficult chip or bunker shot. On the other hand, a well-struck approach shot can leave the ball within birdie range, setting up an excellent opportunity to score.

Approach shots also require a golfer to consider different factors such as the wind, the slope of the green, and the location of the pin. A player must determine the right club, the correct shot shape, and the right distance to hit the ball to ensure that it lands in the right place on the green.

Moreover, approach shots require a golfer to have excellent ball-striking ability. To hit a good approach shot, a golfer must hit the ball cleanly with the correct amount of backspin, which helps the ball stop quickly on the green. A good approach shot also requires a golfer to hit the ball with the right trajectory to ensure that it carries the necessary distance and stops on the green without rolling too far.

In summary, approach shots are critical to scoring well in golf, and golfers must spend adequate time and effort practicing them. They require accuracy, distance control, and an ability to factor in various factors such as wind and slope of the green. In the following chapters, we will dive deeper into how to hit good approach shots, the different types of approach shots, and how to practice them effectively.

Different Types of Approach Shots

Approach shots are an integral part of golf and are often what separate good golfers from great ones. Approach shots are defined as any shot played from over 100 yards out that is intended to land on or near the green. There are several types of approach shots that golfers can use, depending on their skill level, the lie of the ball, and the type of shot required.

One of the most common approach shots in golf is the standard pitch shot. This shot is played with a wedge and is used when the golfer is just off the green and needs to land the ball softly on the putting surface. The key to a good pitch shot is to keep the hands and wrists soft, allowing the clubhead to glide under the ball and lift it into the air. A proper pitch shot should land on the green with a low, spinning trajectory and stop quickly.

Another type of approach shot is the high shot. The high shot is similar to the pitch shot but is used when the ball needs to be hit high and land softly. The high shot requires a more open clubface and a steeper swing plane to generate the necessary height and spin. This shot is often used when the golfer needs to carry the ball over a bunker or other obstacle and stop it quickly on the green.

The bump-and-run is a type of approach shot that is played low to the ground and allowed to run out to the hole. This shot is often used when the golfer is just off the green and needs to get the ball close to the hole without risking a miss. The key to a good bump-and-run is to use a club with less loft, such as a 7 or 8 iron, and to make a short, compact swing. The ball should be played back in the stance, and the hands should be kept ahead of the clubhead at impact to promote a low, rolling shot.

The low shot is another type of approach shot that is used when the golfer needs to keep the ball low or avoid obstacles such as trees or overhanging branches. The low shot is played with a shorter backswing and a more compact follow-through, allowing the golfer to control the trajectory of the shot more easily.

In conclusion, approach shots are a critical part of the game of golf, and mastering different types of approach shots is essential for success on the course. By understanding the different types of approach shots and practicing them regularly, golfers can improve their game and increase their chances of success. The key to a good approach shot is to keep the swing smooth, the hands soft, and the focus on the target.

In conclusion, approach shots come in various types, and golfers must be able to execute them effectively to score well. Understanding the different types of approach shots and how to execute them can help golfers make better decisions on the course and improve their chances of scoring well. Practice each type of approach shot to gain more confidence and consistency in your game.

Shot Selection for Approach Shots

One of the most critical skills in golf is the ability to select the right club and shot for each approach to the green. Choosing the wrong club or shot can lead to poor results and costly mistakes. In this chapter, we will discuss shot selection for approach shots and provide tips on how to make the right choice.

1. Assess the situation: The first step in shot selection is to assess the situation. Consider the distance to the green, wind direction and speed, lie of the ball, pin position, and any hazards that need to be avoided. Based on these factors, you can narrow down your club selection and determine the type of shot you need to play.

2. Club selection: Once you have assessed the situation, you need to select the right club. Generally, you want to choose a club that will allow you to hit the green comfortably without risking overshooting or coming up short. The distance to the pin, wind conditions, and your personal strengths and weaknesses all come into play when selecting a club.

3. Shot type: Once you have selected your club, you need to determine the type of shot you want to play. There are several shot types that you can use depending on the situation. These include:

    •   High approach: A high approach shot is used when you need to clear an obstacle like a bunker or water hazard. To hit a high approach shot, use a high-lofted club, like a pitching wedge or sand wedge, and take a full swing. Aim to hit the ball high into the air and land it softly on the green.

- Low approach: A low approach shot is useful when you need to keep the ball under the wind or hit a punch shot under tree branches. To hit a low approach shot, use a low-lofted club, like a 7-iron or 8-iron, and play the ball back in your stance. Make a shorter, controlled swing and hit down on the ball to keep it low.

- Draw/fade: Sometimes, you may need to shape your approach shot to fit the contours of the green. To draw the ball, aim slightly right of the target and swing in-to-out. To fade the ball, aim slightly left of the target and swing out-to-in.

4. Visualize the shot: Once you have selected the club and shot type, take a moment to visualize the shot in your mind. Imagine the flight of the ball, the trajectory, and the landing spot on the green. This visualization can help you execute the shot with confidence and precision.

5. Execute the shot: Finally, it's time to execute the shot. Take a practice swing or two to get a feel for the shot, then step up to the ball and commit to the shot. Keep your focus on your target and make a smooth, controlled swing. Don't let negative thoughts or distractions interfere with your shot.

By following these tips for shot selection, you can improve your approach shots and hit more greens in regulation. Remember, every shot counts, and the right shot selection can make all the difference in your game.

Critical Step - Partial Shots

Approach shots don't always require a full swing with a high-lofted club. Sometimes, a partial shot with a lower-lofted club can be more effective in getting the ball close to the pin. These partial shots can include pitch shots, chip shots, and bump-and-run shots.

Pitch shots are typically used when the ball is in the rough or in a position where you need to carry it over a bunker or hazard. To execute a pitch shot, use a higher-lofted club such as a sand wedge or lob wedge and make a shorter backswing, accelerating through the ball with a steep angle of attack to create backspin and height on the shot.

Chip shots are used when you're closer to the green and have less green to work with. Use a lower-lofted club such as a 7 or 8 iron and make a shorter backswing with a descending blow on the ball to produce a low-trajectory shot that releases on the green.

Bump-and-run shots are used when you have plenty of green to work with, but there may be an obstacle such as a bunker or rough that needs to be navigated. Use a lower-lofted club such as a 5 or 6 iron and play the shot like a putt with a putting grip and stroke. The ball will roll more on the ground and won't get as much air as a pitch or chip shot.

Partial shots require a lot of feel and touch, so it's important to practice them regularly to gain confidence in your ability to execute them. Practice hitting different types of partial shots to various targets to get a better understanding of how the ball will react and how much distance you can expect to get with each shot.

In addition to being effective in certain situations, partial shots can also be a great way to take some pressure off of your full swing. By knowing you have the ability to hit different types of shots, you can be more confident in your ability to get the ball close to the pin, even when the situation may not call for a full swing with a high-lofted club.

Critical Step - Evaluating the Safe Areas in Approach Play

Approach shots in golf require accuracy and precision, but they also require a strategic mindset. One aspect of approach play that is often overlooked is evaluating the safe areas on the green. These are areas where you can miss the green and still have a good chance of getting up and down for par.

Evaluating the safe areas on the green can help you make better decisions when selecting a target for your approach shot. This is especially important when you're facing a difficult approach shot where the margin for error is small.

Here are some factors to consider when evaluating the safe areas on the green:

1. Pin Placement: The position of the pin on the green is a key factor in determining the safe areas. If the pin is located on the left side of the green, for example, you may have a larger safe area on the right side of the green.

2. Slope: The slope of the green can also impact the safe areas. A green that slopes from left to right may have a larger safe area on the left side of the green.

3. Wind: Wind can also impact the safe areas. If you're facing a headwind, for example, you may need to aim further right or left to ensure your ball stays on the green.

4. Hazards: Hazards such as bunkers, water, or trees can impact the safe areas. If there's a bunker guarding the front of the green, you may want to aim for the middle of the green to avoid it.

By evaluating these factors and identifying the safe areas on the green, you can make better decisions when selecting a target for your approach shot. This can lead to more greens hit in regulation and more birdie opportunities.

It's also important to note that evaluating the safe areas on the green requires practice and experience. Spend time on the driving range hitting approach shots to different targets and evaluating the safe areas. Over time, you'll develop a better understanding of where the safe areas are and how to take advantage of them.

Critical Step - Committing to Your Approach Shots

One of the most important aspects of approach shots is committing to the shot you've chosen. Once you've evaluated the situation and decided on the type of shot, you're going to hit, it's important to fully commit to that shot and not second-guess yourself during the swing.

Lack of commitment can lead to indecisiveness and inconsistency in your approach shots. Doubting yourself during the swing can cause you to make changes mid-swing, leading to poor contact and a bad shot. It's important to trust your instincts and be confident in your decision-making.

Commitment also means fully committing to the swing itself. This means making a full, aggressive swing with a positive mindset, rather than a tentative or defensive swing. A full swing will create better contact with the ball, resulting in more distance and accuracy.

To help commit to your approach shots, it's important to have a pre-shot routine that you follow for every shot. This routine can include visualization, practice swings, and deep breaths to help calm the nerves and focus on the shot at hand. By having a consistent routine, you can help build confidence and eliminate doubt in your approach shots.

Another way to commit to your approach shots is to focus on the process rather than the outcome. Instead of worrying about where the ball will end up, focus on the steps you need to take to hit the shot you've chosen. This can help you stay present and, in the moment, rather than getting caught up in the future results.

In conclusion, committing to your approach shots is crucial to achieving success on the golf course. Trust your instincts, have a consistent pre-shot routine, and focus on the process to help build confidence and eliminate doubt. Remember that golf is a game of confidence, and committing to your approach shots can help build that confidence and lead to better results.

DRIVING

CHAPTER 11

The Basics of Driving

Driving the ball in golf is all about technique. A solid foundation of grip, stance, and swing mechanics is essential for driving the ball accurately and with maximum distance. In this chapter, we'll go over the basics of driving technique, with tips and drills to help you improve your form.

Your stance is the foundation of your swing, providing stability and balance throughout the motion. To set up your stance for driving, start by standing with your feet shoulder-width apart and parallel to the target line. The ball should be positioned slightly forward in your stance, closer to your left foot (for right-handed golfers). Your weight should be evenly distributed between your feet, with your knees flexed slightly. This helps create a stable base for your swing and allows for a full range of motion.

Swing Mechanics

The swing is the heart of driving, and proper mechanics are essential for a successful shot. Here are the basic steps of a proper swing:

1. Takeaway - Begin by slowly and smoothly moving the club back from the ball, keeping your left arm straight and your wrists firm.

2. Backswing - Continue the backswing, rotating your shoulders and hips to create torque and tension in your body.

3. Downswing - Initiate the downswing by shifting your weight onto your left foot (for right-handed golfers) and using your lower body to start the motion.

4. Impact - As you approach the ball, focus on making solid contact and keeping your head steady.

5. Follow-through - Finish your swing with a smooth follow-through, extending your arms and club toward the target and finishing in a balanced position.

Playing Shots with Different Trajectories with a Driver

Being able to hit the driver with different trajectories can be a useful skill on the golf course. In this chapter, we'll discuss how to adjust your swing to hit the driver with a high, medium, or low trajectory.

High Trajectory

To hit the driver with a high trajectory, you'll want to focus on two things - tee height and swing path. First, tee the ball up higher than normal to create a higher launch angle. Then, on your downswing, focus on swinging up on the ball with a slightly more upward swing path. This will help you hit the ball high and maximize your carry distance.

Medium Trajectory

For a medium trajectory with the driver, focus on a neutral tee height and swing path. This means teeing the ball up at a normal height and swinging the club on a neutral or slightly upward path. The goal is to hit the ball straight and maximize your distance without sacrificing accuracy.

Low Trajectory

To hit the driver with a low trajectory, you'll want to tee the ball lower than normal and focus on a more downward swing path. This will help you hit the ball low and create more roll on the fairway. Keep in mind that hitting the ball too low can result in a lack of carry distance, so it's important to find the right balance.

When adjusting your swing for different trajectories, it's important to maintain good swing mechanics and avoid making drastic changes to your swing. Focus on making small adjustments to your tee height and swing path to achieve the desired trajectory.

It's also worth noting that wind conditions can play a significant role in the trajectory of your driver shots. When playing in windy conditions, adjust your tee height and swing path accordingly to counteract the effects of the wind and achieve the desired trajectory.

In summary, being able to adjust your driver trajectory can be a useful skill on the golf course. Experiment with different tee heights and swing paths to find the optimal trajectory for your swing and course conditions.

Critical Step - Tee Height with the Driver

When it comes to hitting the driver, the height of the tee can have a significant impact on the ball flight and distance. In this chapter, we'll discuss the importance of tee height with the driver and how to find the optimal tee height for your swing.

The first thing to consider is the size of the clubhead on your driver. If you have a larger clubhead, you'll want to tee the ball higher to ensure that you're making contact with the sweet spot of the clubface. On the other hand, if you have a smaller clubhead, teeing the ball too high can result in pop-ups or high, weak shots.

The next factor to consider is your swing. If you have a steep swing, you'll want to tee the ball higher to ensure that you're hitting up on the ball and creating the optimal launch angle for maximum distance. If you have a flatter swing, teeing the ball lower can help you make solid contact and avoid hitting the ball too high.

So, how do you find the right tee height for your swing? Here's a simple method:

1. Start by teeing the ball at a medium height, roughly halfway up the clubface.

2. Hit a few shots and pay attention to the ball flight and distance.

3. If the ball flight is too low and you're not getting enough distance, try teeing the ball higher.

4. If the ball flight is too high and you're losing distance, try teeing the ball lower.

5. Experiment with different tee heights until you find the optimal height for your swing.

It's important to note that the optimal tee height can vary from player to player, so don't be afraid to experiment to find what works best for you. And remember, tee height is just one factor in hitting the driver - make sure you're also focusing on your setup, swing mechanics, and course management to maximize your driving performance.

Drawing and Fading the Ball with the Driver

One of the most exciting aspects of driving in golf is the ability to shape your shots. By intentionally curving the ball in flight, you can navigate around obstacles, land on the best side of the fairway, or add distance to your shots. The two most common types of shot shaping are the draw and the fade.

The draw is a shot that curves from right to left (for right-handed players) in flight. It's achieved by swinging slightly from the inside-out, which imparts a clockwise spin on the ball. The result is a shot that starts right of the target and curves back towards it.

The fade, on the other hand, is a shot that curves from left to right in flight. It's achieved by swinging slightly from the outside-in, which imparts a counter clockwise spin on the ball. The result is a shot that starts left of the target and curves away from it.

Both the draw and fade can be useful shots to have in your arsenal, and the key to hitting them consistently is to understand the mechanics behind them. Here are some tips for hitting both shots with your driver:

Drawing the Ball

1. Aim slightly right of your target.

2. Take a slightly closed stance, with your feet and shoulders aimed slightly left of the target.

3. Swing slightly from the inside-out, keeping your clubface square to the target at impact.

4. Follow through towards your target, with your hands and arms rotating through the shot.

Fading the Ball

1. Aim slightly left of your target.

2. Take a slightly open stance, with your feet and shoulders aimed slightly right of the target.

3. Swing slightly from the outside-in, keeping your clubface square to the target at impact.

4. Follow through away from your target, with your hands and arms rotating through the shot.

It's important to practice both shots on the range before trying them on the course. By developing a consistent technique for each shot, you can add a new dimension to your driving game and improve your overall score.

Critical Step - Why Most Pros Only Fade the Ball with Their Driver

As we discussed in the previous chapter, there are two common types of shot shaping in golf - the draw and the fade. However, if you watch professional golfers on television, you'll notice that the vast majority of them use a fade with their driver. But why is that?

There are a few reasons why most pros prefer to hit a fade off the tee:

1.   Control: A fade is a more predictable shot than a draw. It's easier to control the distance and trajectory of a fade, which is important when hitting long drives on tight fairways.

2.   Accuracy: A fade generally lands softer and stops quicker than a draw. This means that a fade is more likely to stay on the fairway and not run through into the rough or other hazards.

3.   Consistency: Hitting a consistent fade with the driver is easier than hitting a consistent draw. It requires less adjustment and timing to execute, which can lead to more consistent results.

4.   Natural Swing: For many golfers, a fade is a more natural shot than a draw. It's easier to align the body and square up the clubface when swinging from outside-in, which is the ideal swing path for a fade.

Of course, there are exceptions to this rule. Some golfers prefer to hit a draw, and they can be just as successful with it as those who hit a fade. However, for the vast majority of golfers, hitting a consistent fade with the driver is the preferred choice.

If you're struggling with your driving and want to improve your consistency and accuracy off the tee, consider working on your fade. With practice and patience, you can develop a reliable and effective shot that will help you lower your scores and enjoy the game even more.

Course Management with the Driver

Hitting long drives is an important part of golf, but it's not just about distance. It's also about course management - knowing when to hit your driver and when to play a safer shot. In this chapter, we'll discuss some tips for using your driver wisely on the course.

1.   Know the course: Before you start your round, take some time to study the layout of the course. Look for hazards, such as bunkers and water, and identify where you can safely hit your driver. Plan your tee shots accordingly.

2.   Play to your strengths: If you're not a long hitter, don't try to force it with your driver. Instead, play to your strengths and hit a club that you're comfortable with. This might mean hitting a 3-wood or even a hybrid off the tee on certain holes.

3.   Take risks strategically: There may be times when it makes sense to take a risk with your driver, such as when you need to make up ground or take

advantage of a favourable wind. However, be strategic about it. Don't take unnecessary risks that could lead to trouble.

4. Use your driver as a weapon: On some holes, your driver can be a weapon that helps you set up birdie opportunities. Look for holes where a well-placed drive can give you a short approach shot and be aggressive with your driver when the situation calls for it.

5. Don't be afraid to lay up: Sometimes the smart play is to lay up short of a hazard or other obstacle. This can be a tough decision, especially if you're feeling confident with your driver, but it's often the best way to avoid trouble and keep your score on track.

By using your driver wisely and playing to your strengths, you can improve your course management and make better decisions off the tee. Remember, it's not just about hitting long drives - it's about hitting smart shots that set you up for success on the rest of the hole.

Critical Step - When Y/ou Should Consider Using Your 3 Wood Over Your Driver

The driver is often seen as the most glamorous club in the bag, but sometimes it makes sense to leave it in the bag and reach for your 3 wood instead. In this chapter, we'll discuss some situations were using your 3 wood off the tee might be a better option than your driver.

1. Accuracy over distance: If accuracy is more important than distance on a particular hole, then using your 3 wood off the tee might be the best option. A well-struck 3 wood can travel a good distance but with more control and accuracy than a driver.

2. Narrow fairways: If the fairway is narrow and there's trouble on both sides, using your 3 wood can be a safer play. It might not give you as much distance as the driver, but it will give you more control and accuracy.

3. Windy conditions: When it's windy, using your 3 wood can be a better option than your driver. The lower ball flight of the 3 wood can help keep the ball under the wind and result in a straighter shot.

4. Dogleg holes: When you're faced with a dogleg hole, using your 3 wood can be a better option than your driver. A well-placed 3 wood can help you position the ball to take advantage of the turn in the fairway.

5. Trouble off the tee: If there's trouble, such as a hazard or out-of-bounds, close to the fairway, using your 3 wood can be a safer play than your driver. This can help you avoid big numbers on the scorecard and keep your round on track.

By understanding when to use your 3 wood off the tee, you can improve your course management and make better decisions on the course. Remember, it's not just about hitting the longest shot - it's about hitting the smartest shot that sets you up for success on the rest of the hole.

QUALITY PRACTICE

CHAPTER 12

Critical Step - Quality vs Quantity of Practice in Golf

Practice is essential in golf to improve skills, enhance technique, and develop consistency. However, the quality of practice is just as important as the quantity. Many golfers make the mistake of thinking that practicing for hours every day is the only way to improve. Practicing for a shorter period but with focus and purpose can yield more significant results. In this chapter, we'll explore the differences between quality and quantity of practice and provide tips on how to maximize your practice sessions.

Quantity of Practice

Quantity of practice refers to the amount of time spent practicing. Many golfers believe that the more time they spend practicing, the better they will become. While it is true that practice is essential, too much of it can lead to burnout, injuries, and frustration. Over-practicing can also lead to a decline in performance, as the body and mind can become fatigued.

Quality of Practice

Quality of practice refers to the effectiveness of the practice session. Quality practice involves focused and purposeful practice, with the goal of improving a specific aspect of your game. For example, if you're struggling with your short game, quality practice would involve dedicating your time to working on your chipping, pitching, and bunker shots.

Quality practice is just as important as quantity when it comes to improving your golf game. By setting specific goals, limiting distractions, and practicing with a purpose, you can maximize the effectiveness of your practice sessions. Remember to take breaks, mix up your routine, and focus on technique. With consistent quality practice, you can improve your skills, develop consistency, and lower your scores on the course.

Maximizing Effectiveness of Practice Sessions

Practice is a crucial component of improving your golf game. By practicing regularly and effectively, you can develop your skills, build your confidence, and ultimately perform better on the course. In this chapter, we will explore some key strategies for practicing effectively and improving your game.

Set Goals

One of the most important things you can do to improve your golf game is to set clear and specific goals for yourself. Your goals should be realistic and achievable, but also challenging enough to motivate you to improve. Set goals for specific aspects of your game, such as driving distance or accuracy, short game proficiency, or putting consistency./

Create a Practice Plan

Once you have set your goals, it's important to create a practice plan that will help you achieve them. Your practice plan should be structured and well-organized, with a clear focus on the areas of your game that need the most improvement. Incorporate a variety of drills and exercises into your practice routine and be sure to practice both on the range and on the course.

Focus on Quality over Quantity

When it comes to practice, quality is more important than quantity. It's better to spend a focused hour practicing with a specific goal in mind than to spend several hours mindlessly hitting balls without a plan. Focus on quality over quantity and be intentional about every shot you take.

Get Feedback

Getting feedback is an important part of improving your golf game. Ask a coach, fellow golfer, or use a training aid, to observe your swing and provide constructive feedback. You can also use video analysis to review your swing and identify areas for improvement.

Practice Under Pressure

Finally, it's important to practice under pressure to simulate the experience of playing in a tournament or high-pressure situation. Set up a practice game with a friend or challenge yourself to hit a certain number of shots in a row from a specific distance. This type of pressure can help you develop mental toughness and improve your ability to perform under stress.

Practice is essential to improving your golf game. By setting clear goals, creating a structured practice plan, focusing on quality over quantity, getting feedback, and practicing under pressure, you can develop your skills and build your confidence on the course. In this chapter, we explored key strategies for effective practice, with a focus on goal setting, planning, and feedback. By incorporating these strategies into your practice routine, you can become a more skilled and successful golfer.

The Importance of Balanced Practice

Practice is essential to improve one's game. But how should you distribute your practice time between putting, short game, approach shots, and driving? In this chapter, we will explore the percentage of time you should spend on each aspect of the game to become a well-rounded golfer.

To optimize your practice time and improve your overall game, it's recommended that you divide your practice time into four main areas: putting, short game, approach shots, and driving. Let's take a closer look at how much time you should be dedicating to each area:

Putting

Many experts suggest that you should be spending at least 40-50% of your practice time on putting. Putting is a crucial part of the game, and it's where you can shave the most strokes off your scorecard. Practicing different types of putts, such as long-range putts, uphill putts, downhill putts, and breaking putts, can help you become more confident and consistent on the greens.

Short Game

Around 20-30% of your practice time should be spent on your short game, which includes chipping, pitching, and bunker shots. These shots are critical for getting up and down from around the green and can save you many strokes over the course of a round. Focus on developing different types of shots, such as low runners, high lobs, and spin shots, to help you get the ball close to the pin.

Approach Shots

Around 20-30% of your practice time should be spent on approach shots, which are shots hit from 100-200 yards from the green. These shots are important for giving yourself birdie opportunities and setting up easy par putts. It's important to practice hitting approach shots from different lies and distances, as well as working on accuracy and distance control.

Driving

Around 10-20% of your practice time should be spent on your driver. While it's tempting to spend a lot of time hitting driver shots, it's important to remember that the driver is just one part of the game. Focus on developing a consistent and reliable swing with your driver, and work on hitting fairways rather than just trying to hit the ball as far as possible.

Range Goats vs Course Gofers

Golfers who want to improve their game often debate whether to spend more time practicing at the driving range or playing on the course. Both have their advantages and disadvantages, and the decision depends on the golfer's goals and priorities.

Spending time at the driving range is essential for developing fundamental skills, such as the swing mechanics, ball striking, and distance control. Moreover, the range allows golfers to experiment with different clubs, grips, and swing techniques. It also provides an opportunity to work on specific weaknesses, such as hitting fades or draws, shaping shots, or fixing a slice.

On the other hand, practicing at the driving range can be monotonous and repetitive, lacking the variety and unpredictability of the course. Golfers may get too comfortable hitting from the same lie and direction, and not learn to adapt to the changing terrain, wind, and other elements of the game. Also, hitting balls from a tee or a mat may create unrealistic expectations of how well the shots would perform in a real-life situation.

Playing on the course, on the other hand, allows golfers to apply their skills in a more realistic setting and under pressure. They can experience different lies, hazards, green speeds, and pin positions, and learn how to strategize and manage their game. Moreover, playing with other golfers can provide social interaction, competition, and a chance to observe and learn from others' techniques.

However, playing on the course can be time-consuming and expensive, especially for those who have a busy schedule or limited access to courses. It can also be frustrating for beginners or golfers with inconsistent swings, as they may lose a lot of balls, slow down the pace of play, or get discouraged by poor results.

The ideal approach to practicing golf is to strike a balance between the driving range and the course, depending on the golfer's skill level, goals, and availability. For beginners or those who struggle with the basics, spending more time at the range to develop their swing and ball control is advisable. As their skills improve, they can gradually shift their focus to playing on the course, practicing specific shots, or working on course management and mental game.

In conclusion, practicing golf is a complex and multifaceted process that involves a combination of range work and course play. By understanding the advantages and limitations of each method and balancing them according to their needs, golfers can improve their skills, enjoyment, and overall performance on the course.

My Favourite Practice Drills

Practicing with intention and focus is essential to improve your skills in any sport. Golf is no exception, as it requires a significant amount of dedication and effort to master. In this chapter, we will explore some of the best practice drills in golf that can help you improve your game.

Putting Drills

Putting is one of the most critical aspects of the game and practicing it can lead to significant improvements in your scores. Here are some of the best putting drills:

The Gate Drill

Place two tees on the green, slightly wider than your putter's head. Putt the ball through the gates to improve your accuracy.

The Clock Drill

Place six balls in a circle around the hole, each around 3-5 feet away. Putt each ball to the hole, moving clockwise around the circle. This drill will help you practice different distances and angles.

One-Handed Putting

Practice putting with only one hand to improve your feel and touch on the green.

Short Game Drills

The first step in practicing your short game is to set goals. By setting specific goals, you can focus your practice sessions and measure your progress. Here are some examples of short game goals you can set:

- Improve your chipping accuracy

- Increase your bunker shot success rate

- Lower your putting average

Once you've set your goals and identified the shots you want to practice, it's time to create a practice plan. When practicing your short game, it's important to vary your shots to simulate different course situations. Try practicing different types of chips, pitches, and bunker shots, and practice from different lies and slopes. This will help you develop a wider range of skills and prepare for a variety of course conditions.

Here are some tips for creating an effective short game practice plan:

- Start with a warm-up routine to prepare your body and mind for practice

- Focus on your weakest areas first to give them extra attention

- Spend time on different types of shots to develop a well-rounded short game

- Practice both in the practice area and on the course to simulate game situations

Chipping is a critical part of your short game, and these drills will help you improve your technique and accuracy.

The Coin Drill

Place a coin on the green and practice chipping to the coin. This drill will help you develop your accuracy and control.

The Bucket Drill

Place a bucket on the green, around 10-15 yards away. Try to chip the ball into the bucket, focusing on the correct trajectory and spin.

The Hula Hoop Drill

Place a hula hoop on the green and practice chipping the ball into the hoop from different distances and angles.

Approach Play Drills

Improving your iron play can lead to more accurate approach shots and lower scores. These drills will help you develop your technique and ball striking.

The Alignment Drill

Place two clubs on the ground, pointing towards your target one along your foot line and one along the target line. Practice hitting balls, focusing on aligning your clubface with the target line.

The Divot Drill

Place a towel or piece of paper on the ground behind the ball and practice hitting iron shots, trying to take a divot after the ball. This drill will help you improve your ball-turf contact and strike.

The 3-Club Drill

Practice hitting different iron shots with three clubs, such as a 6-iron, 8-iron, and pitching wedge. This drill will help you develop your ball flight control and distance control.

Draw and Fade

Practise shot shaping by hitting alternate shots, one draw then one fade. Change the club after every 2 shots.

Driving Drills

Driving is a critical part of your game, and improving your technique can lead to more accurate and longer drives. Here are some of the best driving drills:

Here are some drills to help you improve your driving technique:

Grip pressure drill

Place a towel or glove under your left armpit and grip the club as normal. This drill helps you maintain proper grip pressure and keeps your arms and hands in sync.

Alignment stick drill

Place an alignment stick on the ground parallel to your target line and practice swinging over it. This helps you maintain a consistent swing path and prevents slices or hooks.

Weight shift drill

Place a towel or ball under your right foot (for right-handed golfers) and practice shifting your weight onto your left foot during the downswing. This helps you initiate the downswing with your lower body and create more power.

The Headcover Drill

Place a headcover just outside or inside your target line and practice hitting drives, trying to avoid hitting the headcover. This drill will help you improve your accuracy and ball flight control.

The Driver-Wedge Drill

Practice hitting drivers and then immediately hitting a wedge shot. This drill will help you develop your swing tempo and transition between clubs.

By mastering the basics of grip, stance, and swing mechanics, you'll be well on your way to driving the ball accurately and with maximum distance. Practice these techniques and drills regularly to improve your driving performance and take your golf game to the next level.

BRINGING TOGETHER ON THE COURSE

CHAPTER 13

Bringing your practice to the course

Practicing is an essential aspect of golf. However, all that practice can go to waste if you can't perform when it counts. This is where bringing your practice into a competitive situation can help. By simulating a competitive environment during your practice, you can prepare yourself mentally and physically for the real deal.

Here are some tips for bringing your practice into a competitive situation:

Play with a purpose

Don't just hit balls mindlessly on the range. Instead, have a specific goal in mind for each shot you hit. For example, try to hit a certain number of fairways or greens in regulation, or hit a fade or a draw with your shots. This will help you focus your practice and give you a clear objective to work towards.

Play with a friend

Practicing with a friend can make your practice sessions more fun and competitive. You can set up mini-games or challenges for each other, such as trying to hit a certain target or seeing who can make the most putts from a particular distance. This will help you simulate a competitive environment and keep things interesting.

Use pressure drills

Pressure is a big part of competitive golf, so it's important to practice playing under pressure. There are many pressure drills you can use, such as hitting shots with a consequence for missing a target, or trying to make a certain number of putts in a row. These drills can help you get used to performing under pressure and develop mental toughness.

Play on the course

While practicing on the range is important, nothing can simulate the experience of playing on the course. Try to play as many holes as possible during your practice sessions and treat each shot as if you were playing in a real round. This will help you get used to playing under different conditions and develop your course management skills.

Stay positive

Finally, it's important to stay positive during your practice sessions. Don't get too down on yourself if you hit a bad shot or miss a putt. Instead, focus on what you did right and what you can improve on. This positive attitude will help you stay motivated and perform your best when it counts.

In conclusion, bringing your practice into a competitive situation is essential for improving your performance on the course. By playing with a purpose, using pressure drills, and playing on the course, you can prepare yourself mentally and physically for competitive golf. Remember to stay positive and have fun, and you'll be well on your way to achieving your golfing goals.

Playing Competitive Golf Well

Golf can be a challenging sport, and competing in tournaments or other events can add an extra layer of pressure. Whether you're a beginner or a seasoned player, it's essential to develop strategies for playing your best golf in competitive situations. In this chapter, we'll discuss some tips for playing competitive golf well.

Prepare Mentally and Physically

The first step in playing competitive golf well is to prepare mentally and physically. Make sure you have a proper warm-up routine before the event. Get to the course early, practice putting, chipping and take some swings on the driving range to get your body warmed up. Take time to visualize the course and the shots you will need to hit. Prepare a game plan based on your strengths and weaknesses.

Focus on Your Own Game

When playing competitive golf, it's essential to focus on your own game, rather than getting distracted by your competitors. Keep your mind focused on what you need to do to play your best and try not to get caught up in the scores of other players.

Stay Positive

Golf can be a frustrating game, but it's important to stay positive, especially in competitive situations. Keep your attitude upbeat and try to stay calm and relaxed on the course. Remember that mistakes will happen, and it's how you react to them that matters most.

Play Smart

When playing in a tournament or other competitive event, it's crucial to play smart golf. Don't take unnecessary risks or attempt shots that you're not comfortable with. Instead, focus on playing to your strengths and making smart decisions on the course.

Manage Your Emotions

Competitive golf can be an emotional rollercoaster, with highs and lows throughout the round. It's important to manage your emotions and not let them get the best of you. Take deep breaths, stay focused on the present, and don't dwell on the past or worry about the future.

Stick to Your Routine

Finally, it's essential to stick to your routine when playing competitive golf. Whether it's your pre-shot routine, your putting routine, or your overall game plan, try to maintain consistency throughout the round. This will help you stay focused and avoid making unnecessary mistakes.

In conclusion, playing competitive golf well requires mental and physical preparation, staying focused on your own game, staying positive, playing smart, managing your emotions, and sticking to your routine. By following these tips, you'll be well on your way to playing your best golf in any competitive situation.

THE MENTAL GAME

CHAPTER 14

The Mental Game of Golf

In golf, mental strength is just as important as physical ability. The mental game of golf involves developing strategies for maintaining focus, staying calm under pressure, and cultivating a positive attitude on the course. In this chapter, we will explore some key strategies for improving your mental game and performing your best on the course.

Maintaining Focus One of the biggest challenges in golf is staying focused throughout a round. The long, slow pace of the game, combined with the distractions of the course, can make it difficult to maintain concentration. To stay focused, it is important to develop a pre-shot routine that helps you to block out distractions and prepare for each shot. Your routine might involve taking a deep breath, visualizing your shot, or repeating a calming mantra to yourself. By following your routine consistently, you can train your mind to stay focused and avoid distractions.

Staying Calm Under Pressure Another key aspect of the mental game of golf is staying calm under pressure. Whether you are playing in a tournament or simply trying to beat your personal best, the pressure to perform can be intense. To stay calm, it is important to maintain perspective and avoid getting too caught up in the moment. Focus on the process of playing each shot, rather than worrying about the outcome. Remind yourself that golf is just a game, and that your worth as a person is not tied to your performance on the course.

Cultivating a Positive Attitude Finally, a positive attitude can be a powerful tool for success in golf. Golf is a challenging and unpredictable game, and it is easy to get discouraged when things don't go your way. To cultivate a positive attitude, focus on the things that are going well in your game, rather than dwelling on mistakes or missed opportunities. Celebrate small victories, like a well-placed shot or a successful putt, and use these positive experiences to build momentum and confidence.

Conclusion The mental game of golf is a critical aspect of success on the course. By developing strategies for maintaining focus, staying calm under pressure, and cultivating a positive attitude, you can improve your mental strength and enhance your overall performance. In this chapter, we discussed the importance of developing a pre-shot routine, staying perspective, and focusing on the positive aspects of your game. By incorporating these strategies into your game, you can become a mentally strong and successful golfer.

Critical Step - Achieving a Flow State

Have you ever experienced a round of golf where everything seemed to just click? You were hitting shots effortlessly, sinking putts from all over the green, and the game felt easy. This feeling of being "in the zone" or "in flow" is a state of mind where you are completely focused on the task at hand, and everything seems to come naturally.

The concept of flow was first introduced by psychologist Mihaly Csikszentmihalyi, who defined it as a state of complete immersion in an activity. When in flow, you are completely focused on the present moment, with no distractions or concerns about the past or future. This state of mind is often associated with increased creativity, productivity, and performance.

When playing golf, being in a flow state can be incredibly beneficial. You are able to play without overthinking your shots, trusting your instincts and muscle memory to guide your swing. You are completely immersed in the game, with no distractions or negative thoughts creeping in.

So how can you achieve a flow state when playing golf? Here are some tips:

1. Be fully present: When you step up to the ball, focus all your attention on the shot you are about to take. Block out any distractions or negative thoughts and trust your instincts.

2. Trust your swing: You have likely spent hours practicing your swing, so trust that it will guide you when on the course. Don't overthink your swing mechanics, simply let your muscle memory take over.

3. Stay relaxed: Tension and stress can be major barriers to achieving a flow state. Take deep breaths and focus on staying relaxed and loose throughout your round.

4. Embrace the challenge: Golf is a challenging game, but it is also what makes it so rewarding. Embrace the challenge and enjoy the process of trying to improve your game.

5. Stay positive: Negativity and self-doubt can disrupt your flow state. Stay positive and focus on the shots you have already made well, rather than dwelling on any mistakes.

In conclusion, being in a flow state can greatly enhance your performance when playing golf. By being fully present, trusting your swing, staying relaxed, embracing the challenge, and staying positive, you can enter a state of mind where you play your best golf. Remember that achieving flow is a state of mind that can be developed and improved over time, so keep practicing and enjoy the process of becoming a better golfer.

Critical Step - Swing Thoughts in Golf

Golf is a game of focus and concentration. Players must maintain their composure and stay committed to their shots, even under pressure. One way to stay focused is by using swing thoughts. Swing thoughts are simple phrases that help golfers focus on their technique during their swings. Here, we will discuss the importance of swing thoughts and provide some examples of effective swing thoughts to improve your game.

Importance of Swing Thoughts

Swing thoughts help golfers maintain focus and stay committed to their shots. They also help golfers identify and correct problems in their swings. By focusing on specific aspects of their technique, golfers can develop muscle memory and refine their swings.

Effective Swing Thoughts:

1. Stay Connected: Keeping your arms and body connected throughout your swing helps maintain proper swing plane and tempo. Focus on keeping your elbows close together throughout your swing.

2. Slow and Steady: A smooth and slow swing is often more effective than a fast, jerky swing. Focus on maintaining a slow and steady tempo throughout your swing.

3. Be Athletic: Golf is often compared to other sports like baseball and tennis. Remember to stay athletic throughout your swing, with a slight knee bend and relaxed grip.

4. Clubhead Square: Keeping the clubhead square throughout your swing is crucial for accuracy. Focus on keeping the clubface square at address and throughout your swing.

5. Tempo: Maintaining a consistent tempo is important for generating power and accuracy. Focus on maintaining a consistent tempo throughout your swing, from takeaway to follow-through.

6. Finish Strong: A good finish is crucial to a good swing. Focus on following through completely and holding your finish until the ball lands.

7. Visualize: Visualization is an important aspect of golf. Visualize the shot you want to make before you swing and focus on making it a reality.

8. Trust Your Swing: Once you've committed to a shot, trust your swing and let it happen. Don't try to steer the ball or make any last-minute adjustments.

Swing thoughts are best practiced on the driving range or during practice rounds. It is important to identify specific swing thoughts that work for you and to focus on them consistently. Over time, swing thoughts can become second nature, improving your technique and consistency on the course.:

Swing thoughts are an important tool for improving your golf game. They help golfers focus on specific aspects of their technique and develop muscle memory. By practicing effective swing thoughts, you can improve your consistency and accuracy on the course. Remember to stay committed to your shots and trust your swing.

Mental Strategies

Golf is not just a physical game, but also a mental one. Your mental state can have a significant impact on your performance on the course. In this chapter, we will explore some key mental game strategies that can help you improve your focus, manage your emotions, and perform better under pressure.

Visualization

Visualization is a powerful mental tool that can help you improve your golf game. By visualizing your shots and seeing yourself hitting the ball the way you want, you can improve your confidence and performance. Take some time before your round to visualize your shots and see yourself hitting the ball with accuracy and distance.

Positive Self-Talk

Your internal dialogue can have a significant impact on your mental state and performance. Negative self-talk can lead to feelings of self-doubt and anxiety, while positive self-talk can help you stay focused and confident. Try to replace negative thoughts with positive ones and focus on your strengths and accomplishments.

Breathing and Relaxation Techniques

Breathing and relaxation techniques can help you manage your emotions and stay calm under pressure. Take a few deep breaths before each shot to calm your nerves and stay focused. You can also try progressive muscle relaxation or visualization techniques to help you relax and stay focused.

Focus on the Present

Golf is a game that requires you to focus on the present moment. Focusing on past mistakes or future shots can distract you from the task at hand. Try to stay focused on the shot you are currently playing and avoid dwelling on past shots or worrying about future ones.

Develop a Pre-Shot Routine

A pre-shot routine can help you stay focused and centred before each shot. Your routine can include visualizing the shot, taking practice swings, and taking a deep breath. By developing a routine, you can build consistency and confidence in your game.

The mental game is an essential component of playing golf. By incorporating visualization, positive self-talk, breathing and relaxation techniques, focusing on the present, and developing a pre-shot routine, you can improve your focus, manage your emotions, and perform better under pressure. In this chapter, we explored some key mental game strategies that can help you improve your golf game and enjoy the game more fully.

COURSE MANAGEMENT

CHAPTER 15

Critical Section - Course Management 101

In golf, course management refers to the process of making strategic decisions about how to play each hole on the course. A strong course management strategy can help you navigate the course more effectively, avoid hazards, and make the most of your strengths as a golfer.

The first step in developing a course management strategy is to study the course carefully before you begin playing. Look at the layout of each hole, taking note of any hazards, slopes, or other challenges that may affect your play. Consider your own strengths and weaknesses as a golfer and think about how you can use them to your advantage on each hole.

Another key element of course management is club selection. By choosing the right club for each shot, you can maximize your distance and accuracy, while minimizing the risk of mistakes. Consider factors like wind, slope, and elevation when choosing your club, and aim to land your ball in a safe and strategic location on the course.

One of the most important aspects of course management is decision making. Golf is a game of strategy and tactics, and the decisions you make on the course can have a significant impact on your overall performance. Take the time to consider your options on each shot, weighing the risks and rewards of each potential approach.

Finally, it is important to remain flexible and adaptable when playing golf. The course can present unexpected challenges, and your strategy may need to be adjusted on the fly in response to changing conditions. By staying focused, keeping a positive attitude, and remaining open to new approaches, you can improve your course management skills and enhance your overall performance on the course.

Remember to forget About the Previous Hole

One of the most significant mental challenges in golf is the ability to forget about the previous hole and focus on the present shot. Golfers must be able to remain mentally disciplined and focused on each shot, regardless of how they performed on the previous hole.

When a golfer finishes a hole, they must put it behind them and focus on the next shot. This can be easier said than done, as golfers may be tempted to dwell on mistakes or successes from the previous hole. Dwelling on the past can be detrimental to a golfer's mental state and their overall performance.

To forget about the previous hole, golfers must focus on the present moment and the shot they are about to make. This involves taking a deep breath, clearing the mind, and visualizing the shot they want to make. By doing so, golfers can help reduce the mental noise and distractions that can interfere with their shot execution.

Another strategy for forgetting about the previous hole is to maintain a consistent pre-shot routine. A pre-shot routine involves a set of deliberate and repeatable actions that a golfer takes before each shot. This routine can help golfers stay focused and, in the moment, rather than dwelling on the past.

Additionally, it is essential to maintain a positive attitude and avoid getting down on oneself for past mistakes. Golf is a game of ups and downs, and it is inevitable that golfers will make mistakes. It is crucial to maintain a positive attitude and to view each shot as a new opportunity for success.

In conclusion, forgetting about the previous hole is a critical aspect of mental discipline in golf. By focusing on the present moment, maintaining a consistent pre-shot routine, and maintaining a positive attitude, golfers can improve their mental game and their overall performance on the course. By letting go of past mistakes and focusing on the shot at hand, golfers can achieve greater success and ultimately improve their overall score.

Committing to your Hole Strategy

After golfers have selected their shots, the next step in course management is committing to a hole strategy. A hole strategy involves considering the layout of the hole, the position of hazards, and the golfer's strengths and weaknesses in order to determine the optimal path to the green. This chapter will explore the importance of committing to a hole strategy and the various factors that should be considered when developing one.

One of the key elements of developing a hole strategy is identifying the strengths and weaknesses of the golfer's game. For example, if a golfer has a strong driving game, they may choose to hit a driver off the tee to set up a shorter approach shot. On the other hand, if a golfer struggles with their short game, they may choose to lay up short of a hazard to avoid a difficult approach shot.

Another important consideration when developing a hole strategy is the layout of the hole. Golfers must consider the position of hazards, the shape and slope of the fairway, and the location of the green when deciding on the best path to take. They must also consider the pin placement on the green, as this can greatly impact the type of shot that is required.

Course conditions are another factor that should be considered when developing a hole strategy. If the course is playing fast and firm, golfers may choose to hit a lower trajectory shot that will roll out further. On the other hand, if the course is playing wet and soft, golfers may choose to hit a higher trajectory shot that will stop quickly upon landing.

Golfers must also consider their overall game plan and the position on the course when developing a hole strategy. For example, if a golfer is leading the tournament and has a comfortable lead, they may choose to play more conservatively and avoid any unnecessary risks. Alternatively, if a golfer is trailing and needs to make up ground, they may choose to take more risks and play more aggressively.

Perhaps the most important element of committing to a hole strategy is mental focus and confidence. Golfers must be fully committed to their plan and trust their abilities to execute the shots successfully. Doubts and second-guessing can lead to hesitation and poor shot execution.

In conclusion, committing to a hole strategy is a critical component of course management in golf. By considering the layout of the hole, course conditions, personal strengths and weaknesses, and overall game plan, golfers can develop an effective strategy that maximizes their chances of success. By remaining mentally focused and confident, golfers can execute their shots with precision and achieve their desired results.

Shot Selection

Next, we will examine the role of shot selection in course management. Shot selection involves choosing the most appropriate shot for each situation. This includes considering factors such as distance, wind direction and strength, and the lie of the ball. Golfers must also consider their own abilities and limitations when selecting a shot. For example, a golfer who struggles with a fade may opt for a different shot shape that plays to their strengths.

The shot selection process involves evaluating the situation, assessing the available options, and choosing the shot that is most likely to result in a successful outcome. This chapter will explore the various factors that golfers should consider when making shot selections.

First and foremost, golfers must take into account the distance to the target. The distance will dictate the type of shot that is needed and the club that should be used. Golfers must also consider the terrain and the lie of the ball. For example, if the ball is sitting on a steep downslope, a shot with a higher lofted club may be necessary to ensure the ball gets up in the air and travels the necessary distance.

Another important factor to consider is the wind conditions. Wind can have a significant impact on the flight of the ball, so golfers must consider the direction and strength of the wind. Shots that are hit into a headwind will require more club and a lower trajectory, while shots hit with a tailwind may require less club and a higher trajectory.

Golfers must also consider their own abilities and limitations when making shot selections. This includes considering any physical limitations, such as lack of strength or flexibility. Golfers must also consider their own shot tendencies, such as a tendency to hit a fade or draw.

Another critical aspect of shot selection is the location of hazards on the course. Hazards, such as bunkers, water, and trees, can greatly impact the decision-making process. Golfers must decide whether to play aggressively and try to carry the hazard, or whether to play it safe and lay up short of the hazard.

Finally, golfers must consider the situation and their overall course strategy when making shot selections. This includes considering the score, the difficulty of the hole, and the position on the course. For example, if a golfer is playing a difficult hole and has already made a few mistakes, they may choose to play conservatively and aim for the middle of the fairway.

In conclusion, shot selection is a critical aspect of course management in golf. Golfers must consider a variety of factors when making shot selections, including distance, wind conditions, terrain and lie, personal abilities and tendencies, hazards, and overall course strategy. By making informed decisions and selecting the most appropriate shot for each situation, golfers can maximize their chances of success on the course.

Committing and Executing Your Chosen Shot

Once a golfer has selected their shot and developed a hole strategy, the next step in course management is to commit to the chosen shot and execute it with precision. This chapter will explore the importance of committing to a shot and the various factors that can impact shot execution.

Committing to a shot involves fully accepting the chosen shot and visualizing its intended outcome. Doubts or second-guessing can lead to hesitation and poor execution, which can have a significant impact on a golfer's score. To fully commit to a shot, golfers must have confidence in their abilities and trust the strategy that they have developed.

Visualization is a critical aspect of committing to a shot. By visualizing the shot's trajectory and intended landing spot, golfers can mentally prepare themselves for the shot and increase their chances of success. Visualization can also help golfers remain focused and block out distractions or negative thoughts.

Once a golfer has committed to a shot, the next step is execution. Shot execution involves proper setup, alignment, and swing mechanics. Proper setup involves establishing a solid stance and grip and ensuring that the clubface is square to the target. Alignment involves aiming the body and clubface towards the intended target, while swing mechanics involve proper tempo, swing plane, and clubface control.

Course conditions can also impact shot execution. For example, if the course is playing into the wind, golfers may need to adjust their setup and swing mechanics to generate more power and maintain ball flight. Similarly, if the course is playing firm and fast, golfers may need to adjust their setup and swing mechanics to account for the extra roll that their shots will get.

Mental focus and discipline are also critical aspects of shot execution. Golfers must remain focused on the shot and block out any distractions or negative thoughts. They must also remain disciplined in their swing mechanics and resist the temptation to make last-minute adjustments or deviations from their plan.

In conclusion, committing to a shot and executing it with precision is a critical aspect of course management in golf. By fully committing to the shot and visualizing its intended outcome, golfers can increase their confidence and reduce hesitation. By focusing on proper setup, alignment, and swing mechanics, golfers can execute their shots with precision and achieve their desired outcome. By remaining mentally focused and disciplined, golfers can improve their chances of success and ultimately improve their overall score.

Analysing the Outcome of the Shot and Planning the Next

Once a golfer has executed their shot, the next step in course management is to analyse the outcome of the shot and plan their next move accordingly. This chapter will explore the importance of analysing shot outcomes and the various factors that can impact shot analysis and subsequent shot selection.

Analysing the outcome of a shot involves assessing the distance, direction, and lie of the ball after it has come to rest. By understanding these factors, golfers can determine their next move and make informed decisions about their shot selection.

Distance is an essential factor to consider when analysing shot outcomes. If a golfer has hit their shot shorter or longer than anticipated, they must adjust their club selection accordingly for their next shot. Direction is another critical factor to consider, as shots that miss their intended target may require golfers to alter their course strategy or make a more challenging shot to recover.

The lie of the ball is also an important consideration when analysing shot outcomes. The lie can impact the golfer's ability to make a clean contact with the ball and control its trajectory. For example, if the ball has landed in a divot or a bunker, the golfer may need to adjust their shot selection to account for the challenging lie.

Once a golfer has analysed the outcome of their shot, the next step is to plan their next move accordingly. This may involve selecting a different club, adjusting their course strategy, or making a more conservative shot to avoid further trouble. Golfers must make informed decisions based on the information they have gathered and their overall course strategy.

Course conditions can also impact shot analysis and subsequent shot selection. For example, if the course is playing fast and firm, golfers may need to adjust their shot selection to account for extra roll on their shots. Alternatively, if the course is playing soft and wet, golfers may need to adjust their shot selection to account for less roll on their shots.

In conclusion, analysing the outcome of a shot and planning the next move is a critical aspect of course management in golf. By understanding the distance, direction, and lie of the ball, golfers can make informed decisions about their next shot and adjust their course strategy accordingly. By considering course conditions and making smart shot selections, golfers can improve their chances of success and ultimately improve their overall score.

Analysing Your Round When Finished

Analysing your round after it is over is a critical component of course management in golf. It involves looking back at your performance, identifying areas where you excelled, and areas where you struggled. By analysing your round, you can gain insight into your strengths and weaknesses, which can help you make better decisions on the course in the future.

The first step in analysing your round is to review your scorecard. This will give you an overall view of how you performed and where you may have made mistakes. You can also review any notes you made during the round, such as the club you used for a particular shot or the direction of the wind.

Next, you should break down your round into smaller parts, such as the front nine and back nine. This will allow you to identify patterns in your game, such as whether you played better on the front or back nine. You can also analyse your performance on individual holes, particularly the ones where you struggled.

When analysing your round, it is important to be honest with yourself about your performance. It can be tempting to blame external factors, such as the weather or the course conditions, but ultimately, you are responsible for your own performance. By being honest about your weaknesses, you can work to improve them and become a better golfer.

Once you have identified areas where you struggled, it is time to develop a plan to improve. This may involve working on your swing, practicing specific shots, or making changes to your course management strategy. It is also important to celebrate your successes and identify areas where you excelled. This will give you the confidence and motivation to continue to improve.

In conclusion, analysing your round after it is over is an important part of course management in golf. It involves reviewing your scorecard, breaking down your round into smaller parts, being honest about your weaknesses, and developing a plan to improve. By analysing your round, you can gain insight into your strengths and weaknesses, which can help you make better decisions on the course in the future.

FITNESS & NUTRITION

CHAPTER 16

Rising Importance

Golf is a sport that has traditionally been associated with finesse and skill rather than raw physical strength. However, in recent years, there has been a growing recognition of the importance of strength training and nutrition in golf.

Strength training involves the use of resistance exercises to build muscular strength and endurance. This type of training can help golfers to improve their swing, increase their clubhead speed, and reduce the risk of injury. Additionally, strength training can help golfers to maintain their strength and fitness as they age, which is particularly important for golfers who wish to continue playing at a high level into their senior years.

Nutrition also plays a crucial role in golf performance. Golfers need to fuel their bodies with the right nutrients to maintain their energy levels, focus, and stamina throughout a round of golf. Proper nutrition can also help golfers to recover from training and competition, reduce inflammation, and prevent injury.

One of the main benefits of strength training for golfers is improved swing mechanics. The golf swing involves a complex series of movements that require strength, stability, and mobility. Stronger muscles can help golfers to maintain the correct posture and alignment throughout the swing, generating more power and accuracy. Furthermore, strength training can help golfers to increase their clubhead speed, which is essential for hitting longer shots.

Another key benefit of strength training for golfers is injury prevention. Golfers are at risk of developing injuries to the back, shoulders, and wrists due to the repetitive nature of the sport. Strength training can help to strengthen the muscles and joints in these areas, reducing the risk of injury and allowing golfers to play pain-free.

In addition to strength training, nutrition is also an essential component of golf performance. Golfers need to consume a balanced diet that provides them with the energy and nutrients they need to perform at their best. A diet that is high in whole foods, such as fruits, vegetables, lean protein, and whole grains, can help golfers to maintain their energy levels throughout a round of golf. Additionally, proper hydration is crucial for golfers, as dehydration can lead to fatigue and decreased performance.

In conclusion, the rising importance of strength training and nutrition in golf reflects a growing recognition of the role that physical fitness plays in sports performance. By incorporating strength training and proper nutrition into their training regimen, golfers can improve their swing mechanics, increase their clubhead speed, reduce the risk of injury, and maintain their performance as they age.

Golf is a physically demanding sport that requires strength, flexibility, and endurance. Proper fitness and nutrition can help you improve your performance, prevent injury, and stay energized on the course. In this chapter, we will explore some key fitness and nutrition strategies for golfers.

Fitness Improving your fitness level can help you develop strength, flexibility, and endurance that are essential for playing golf. Some key fitness exercises for golfers include:

- Core exercises such as planks, crunches, and Russian twists

- Cardiovascular exercises such as jogging, cycling, and swimming.

- Weight training exercises such as squats, lunges, and shoulder presses

- Flexibility exercises such as yoga, stretching, and foam rolling.

Incorporating these exercises into your fitness routine can help you improve your overall fitness level and golf performance.

Nutrition Proper nutrition is essential for staying energized and focused on the course. Some key nutrition strategies for golfers include:

- Staying hydrated by drinking plenty of water before, during, and after your round

- Eating a balanced diet that includes protein, carbohydrates, and healthy fats.

- Avoiding sugary and processed foods that can lead to energy crashes.

- Eating small, frequent meals throughout the day to maintain energy levels.

- Avoiding alcohol and caffeine, which can dehydrate you and affect your performance.

By incorporating these nutrition strategies into your routine, you can stay energized and focused on the course.

Conclusion Fitness and nutrition are essential components of playing golf. By improving your fitness level through core exercises, cardiovascular exercises, weight training, and flexibility exercises, you can improve your golf performance and prevent injury. By following proper nutrition strategies, you can stay energized and focused on the course. In this chapter, we explored some key fitness and nutrition strategies for golfers that can help you improve your golf game and enjoy the game more fully.

Sample exercise plan

An exercise plan for golfers should focus on building strength, increasing flexibility, and improving cardiovascular endurance. The following is a sample exercise plan that includes exercises designed to improve golf performance:

1. Warm-up (5-10 minutes) Start with a few minutes of light cardio, such as jogging, cycling, or jumping jacks. Follow this with some dynamic stretching, such as leg swings, arm circles, and walking lunges.

- Strength Training (20-30 minutes) Include exercises that target the muscles used in the golf swing, such as the core, shoulders, back, and legs. Examples of exercises to include in your strength training routine are

Squats, Deadlifts, Lunges, Step-ups, Push-ups, Rows, Lat pulldowns, Planks, Russian twists

Perform each exercise for 3-4 sets of 8-12 repetitions, using a weight that is challenging but manageable.

- Flexibility Training (10-15 minutes) Golfers need to have a good range of motion to achieve a full backswing and follow-through. Flexibility exercises can help to improve mobility and reduce the risk of injury. Examples of flexibility exercises include Shoulder stretches, Trunk rotations, Hamstring stretches, Hip stretches, Calf stretches

Perform each stretch for 30 seconds to 1 minute on each side.

- Cardiovascular Training (20-30 minutes) Aerobic exercise can improve cardiovascular endurance, which is important for maintaining energy levels throughout a round of golf. Examples of cardiovascular exercises include Jogging, Cycling, Swimming, Rowing, Elliptical machine.

Perform your chosen cardiovascular exercise for 20-30 minutes at a moderate intensity.

5. Cool-down (5-10 minutes) Finish your workout with some gentle stretching and foam rolling to help reduce muscle soreness and promote recovery.

It's important to note that golfers should consult with a fitness professional or coach to create a personalized exercise plan that considers their individual needs, abilities, and limitations. Additionally, golfers should gradually increase the intensity and volume of their exercise program over time to avoid injury and promote long-term progress.

ETIQUETTE AND RULES

CHAPTER 17

Rules of engagement

Golf is a game that is steeped in tradition and etiquette. Understanding and following the rules of golf is essential for playing the game safely, fairly, and respectfully. In this chapter, we will explore some key aspects of golf etiquette and rules, including course etiquette, pace of play, and common rules of the game.

The rules of golf can be daunting for many reasons. Firstly, there are a lot of them. The official rules of golf are over 200 pages long, and while not all of them apply to every situation, it can be overwhelming to try to learn and remember them all. Even the simplified versions of the rules can still seem complex and difficult to understand for beginners.

Another reason the rules of golf may be daunting is that they are often enforced with great seriousness and precision. Unlike many other sports, golf is largely self-regulated, meaning that players are responsible for enforcing the rules themselves. This puts a lot of pressure on players to know the rules and to make sure they are following them correctly. In addition, golf is a sport where even the smallest infraction can result in a penalty, which can be frustrating and discouraging for players who are trying to learn the game.

Finally, the rules of golf can be daunting because they can be difficult to interpret and apply in real-world situations. Golf courses are not always perfectly maintained, and conditions can vary greatly from course to course and even from hole to hole. This means that players may encounter situations that are not covered by the standard rules, or that require interpretation and judgment calls. For example, a ball that comes to rest in a divot on the fairway may be considered a "rub of the green" and require the player to play it as it lies, while a ball that lands in a puddle of water may be considered a "casual water hazard" and allow the player to take a free drop.

All of these factors can make the rules of golf seem daunting and overwhelming, especially for beginners or players who are not familiar with the nuances of the game. However, it's important to remember that the rules of golf are there to ensure fairness and consistency in the game, and that they are an essential part of the sport. While they may be difficult to learn and apply at first, with practice and experience, players can become more comfortable with the rules and better able to navigate the complexities of the game.

Please note: Although this section aims to simplify the rules. It is important to note that if you are playing competitive golf, you should study the rulebook before entering the competition, to ensure both yourself and your playing partners create a level playing field. You should also check the local rules in play at the course as these can change depending on the course conditions.

Course Etiquette

Course etiquette involves following a set of unwritten rules that govern player behaviour on the course. Some key aspects of course etiquette include:

- Following the dress code of the course or facility you are playing on.

- Repairing divots and ball marks on the green

- Raking bunkers after hitting out of them

- Avoiding unnecessary damage to the course

- Remove ball from ground under repair (GIR), normally these areas are clearly marked.

- Being respectful of other players and their shots

- Keeping noise and distractions to a minimum

- Avoiding slow play

Common Rules of the Game

Golf has a set of rules that govern player behaviour on the course. Understanding and following these rules is essential for playing the game fairly and safely. Some common rules of the game include:

- Counting all strokes, including penalties and lost balls

- Taking a drop when your ball is lost or unplayable.

- Playing the ball as it lies, except in certain circumstances.

- Taking a penalty for hitting the ball out of bounds or into a water hazard

- Following specific procedures for relief from obstacles or abnormal ground conditions

Simplifying the rules

Golf etiquette and rules are essential components of playing the game safely, fairly, and respectfully. In this chapter, we explored some key aspects of course etiquette, pace of play, and common rules of the game. By following these guidelines and rules, you can help to ensure a positive and enjoyable experience for all players on the course.

Here is a basic explanation of each of the most essential rules of golf:

Play the ball as it lies, except when allowed to lift, drop, or place the ball under specific rules.

This rule means that you must play your ball from wherever it comes to rest on the course, unless the rules allow you to take a free drop, lift and place the ball, or take a penalty stroke.

Tee your ball within the teeing area at the start of each hole, with no part of the ball outside the teeing area.

This rule means that you must tee your ball within the designated teeing area at the start of each hole, with no part of the ball outside the boundaries of the teeing area.

Play the course as you find it and do not improve your lie, area of intended stance, or swing by moving or pressing down anything growing or fixed.

This rule means that you must play the course as it is and not try to improve your lie or the area where you intend to take your stance or swing by moving anything growing or fixed on the course.

If your ball goes out of bounds, take a one-stroke penalty and play a new ball from where you last played.

This rule means that if your ball goes out of bounds, you must take a one-stroke penalty and play a new ball from where you last played.

If your ball is lost, take a one-stroke penalty, and play another ball from where you last played.

This rule means that if you cannot find your ball, you must take a one-stroke penalty and play another ball from where you last played.

If your ball is in a hazard (i.e., water or bunker), you may not ground your club before making a stroke. Take a one-stroke penalty if you do.

This rule means that if your ball is in a hazard, you cannot touch the ground with your club before making a stroke at the ball. If you do, you must take a one-stroke penalty.

Do not play until the group in front is out of range.

This rule means that you should not hit your ball until the group in front of you is out of range. This is to ensure the safety of other players on the course.

Repair any divots and ball marks made on the green by you or others.

This rule means that you should repair any divots or ball marks made on the green by you or other players on the course.

Record your score accurately and honestly.

This rule means that you should keep an accurate score of your round and report it honestly. Cheating or falsifying your score is not allowed in golf.

Pace of Play

Pace of play is an important consideration in golf. Slow play can create frustration and inconvenience for other players on the course. Some tips for maintaining a good pace of play include:

- Being ready to hit when it's your turn.

- Limiting practice swings and pre-shot routines

- Walking briskly between shots

- Being aware of the group in front of you and allowing faster groups to play through

THE TAKEAWAYS

CHAPTER 18

Golf is a game that has captured the hearts and minds of millions of people around the world for centuries. From its early origins as a simple pastime for shepherds hitting rocks into rabbit holes to the high-tech, competitive sport we know today, golf has evolved in many ways but has always maintained its unique appeal.

For many golfers, the allure of the game lies in the challenge it presents. The constant striving for improvement and the satisfaction of achieving even small successes on the course can be incredibly rewarding. Golf is also a great way to socialize with friends and family, to enjoy the beauty of the outdoors, and to challenge oneself physically and mentally.

But perhaps what makes golf truly special is the way it brings people together. Golf is a game that can be enjoyed by people of all ages, backgrounds, and abilities, and it is a great equalizer. On the golf course, everyone is on a level playing field, and it is often the case that the least likely player will come out on top.

As we have explored in this book, golf is a game that requires both physical and mental skills, and the best players are those who can master both. However, even if we never become experts at the game, we can all find enjoyment and fulfilment in simply striving to improve and learning from our mistakes.

In the end, the game of golf is much more than just a sport. It is a way of life, a source of joy and frustration, and a reflection of the human spirit. Whether we are seasoned pros or beginners just starting out, we can all appreciate the unique and timeless appeal of this wonderful game.

In conclusion, golf is a unique and challenging sport that requires dedication, patience, and a constant desire to improve. Through this book, we have explored the history of the game, the fundamentals, the mental side of golf, and the importance of the right equipment.

We have dived into the intricacies of putting, short game, approach shots, and driving the ball. We have learned that effective practice involves quality over quantity, and that it is important to focus on specific areas that need improvement rather than just hitting ball after ball on the range.

Furthermore, we have simplified the rules and etiquette of the game, making it more accessible and less daunting for beginners. We have explored different grips for the short game and the impact of different shaft flexes, grip sizes, and club designs.

Above all, we have come to appreciate the game of golf for its ability to challenge us physically, mentally, and emotionally. It teaches us patience, discipline, and perseverance, while providing a great way to enjoy the outdoors and socialize with others.

What I hope you take away from this book:

- Gripping the golf club is crucial for controlling the clubface, accuracy, distance, and reducing injury risk. The grip can be broken down into two hands: the lead hand and the trail hand. The lead hand should grip the club in the fingers, while the trail hand should grip the club in the palm. The thumb should rest slightly off-centre for both hands.

- It is important to focus on the trail palm facing the target to ensure a square clubface at impact for generating power and accuracy. The grip pressure should be consistent with both hands throughout the swing, not too tight or too loose, to avoid restricting movement and errant shots.
- Grip pressure and wrist position are crucial to a successful golf swing. A consistent grip pressure with both hands is necessary to prevent restricted movement or slipping.
- Straightening the lead wrist at address can cause the clubface to open, leading to a slice.
- Flaring your feet can significantly impact your swing, and it takes time to perfect.
- A smooth swing is essential for power, consistency, injury prevention, and relaxation on the course.
- The width of a golf swing is the amount of extension and separation between the arms and body during the backswing and downswing. It is crucial for generating power and maintaining accuracy.
- Putting requires a positive mindset, focus, attention to detail, and the ability to manage emotions and practice under pressure.
- Putting from off the green can also be useful, and golfers should assess the lie of the ball, choose the right putter, use a pendulum stroke, aim for the fringe, use the slope, and practice regularly.
- Wrist angles are essential for hitting wedge shots with the right amount of spin, trajectory, distance, and direction. Golfers must maintain the proper wrist angles to control their shots.
- The most important aspect of approach shots is distance control. Being able to consistently hit shots of the desired distance is essential for success on the course. To improve your distance control, it's important to develop a feel for the distance of your shots and to practice with a variety of clubs and distances.
- Approach shots require a strong mental game. This means staying focused, managing your emotions, and committing to your shot selection.
- The optimal tee height can vary from player to player, and it is essential to experiment to find what works best for you.
- Two common types of shot shaping in golf are the draw and the fade. Professional golfers mostly use a fade with their driver. If you're struggling with your driving and want to improve your consistency and accuracy off the tee, consider working on your fade.
- Sometimes it is better to leave the driver in the bag and reach for your 3 wood instead. Understanding when to use your 3 wood off the tee can improve your course management and make better decisions on the course.
- To improve in golf, quality of practice is as important as quantity, and shorter, focused practice sessions can yield better results.
- Being in a flow state or "in the zone" where you're completely focused on the game can be beneficial, as it allows you to play without overthinking your shots.
- Effective swing thoughts can also help improve consistency and accuracy by focusing on specific aspects of technique and developing muscle memory.

- Develop a course management strategy, study the course layout, identify hazards, and consider your own strengths and weaknesses as a golfer.
- Effective shot selection is crucial in golf and involves carefully evaluating the situation, assessing available options, and selecting the shot that is most likely to result in a successful outcome.
- Once the shot has been executed, it's important to analyse its outcome and plan the next move accordingly.
- Finally, be obsessive about improvement analyse each round of golf you have and learn from what you did well and what you need to improve.

So, whether you are a seasoned golfer or just starting out, I hope this book has provided you with valuable insights and tips to help you improve your game and enjoy the sport to the fullest. Remember, golf is a journey, not a destination, and the more you practice and learn, the more you will love this amazing game. Play well.

Made in the USA
Middletown, DE
07 July 2023

34651248R10062